SysAdmin Tools and Protocols: NFS, Cron, Sysctl, and Daemon

James Relington

DEDICATION

To those who seek knowledge, inspiration, and new perspectives—
may this book be a companion on your journey, a spark for curiosity,
and a reminder that every page turned is a step toward discovery.

AKNOWLEDGEMENTS

I would like to express my deepest gratitude to everyone who contributed to the creation of this book. To my colleagues and mentors, your insights and expertise have been invaluable. A special thank you to my family and friends for their unwavering support and encouragement throughout this journey.

NFS: Introduction and Overview

Network File System (NFS) is a protocol that allows a computer to access files over a network in a manner similar to how local storage is accessed. It is widely used in Unix-like operating systems, such as Linux, FreeBSD, and macOS, but has also seen implementations in other environments, making it a universal solution for network-based file sharing. NFS enables a system to mount remote directories from another computer, allowing it to interact with files stored on a different system as if they were part of its own local file system. This capability is a cornerstone for building distributed systems, managing network storage, and streamlining collaborative work environments across multiple machines.

Originally developed by Sun Microsystems in 1984, NFS has evolved significantly over the years, with multiple versions introducing improvements in performance, security, and scalability. The protocol was designed to make remote file access as transparent as possible, minimizing the complexity for end users and administrators. With NFS, a user on one machine can seamlessly read, write, and modify files located on another machine without needing to worry about the underlying network infrastructure. The simplicity of the protocol, combined with its robust features, has made it an essential tool in many IT environments, from small businesses to large-scale enterprise systems.

The primary function of NFS is to provide a way for clients to access files located on a remote server. This is achieved through a client-server model, where the server hosts the files, and the client makes requests for those files over the network. Once the connection is established, the client can interact with the remote files as if they were stored locally. This is particularly useful in environments where multiple machines need to access the same set of data or where data needs to be centralized for easier management and backup.

NFS operates by using Remote Procedure Calls (RPCs) to allow the client to request file operations, such as reading or writing data, from the server. The server, in turn, processes the requests and returns the necessary data or acknowledges the completion of the task. This system allows NFS to abstract the complexities of file systems, presenting a uniform interface to clients regardless of the underlying storage technology. The protocol works by allowing the client to mount a directory from the server, meaning that the remote file system appears as part of the local system's directory structure.

One of the reasons NFS has been so successful is its support for both simple and complex networking environments. Whether it's a small office network with a handful of computers or a large data center with thousands of machines, NFS can scale to meet the needs of both scenarios. The flexibility of NFS is further enhanced by its ability to run over different transport protocols, such as UDP and TCP, allowing administrators to choose the best transport method based on their specific requirements. NFS can also be used in conjunction with other technologies, such as distributed file systems and storage area networks, to provide an even higher level of performance and availability.

Another important aspect of NFS is its support for file locking. This feature ensures that multiple clients do not try to modify the same file simultaneously, which could lead to data corruption. NFS provides mechanisms for file locking, allowing administrators to configure locks at the file or record level. These locks prevent other clients from making conflicting changes, ensuring data consistency and reliability in multi-user environments.

Despite its strengths, NFS is not without its limitations. One of the most notable challenges with NFS is its reliance on a trusted network. Since NFS typically does not encrypt data, it can be vulnerable to security risks if not properly configured. Sensitive data can potentially be intercepted or tampered with during transmission, especially when used over untrusted networks such as the internet. Over time, however, several security mechanisms have been introduced to address these concerns, including Kerberos authentication, which provides strong authentication for both the server and the client, and NFS version 4, which includes built-in support for stronger security features, such as support for Transport Layer Security (TLS) and the use of more advanced encryption methods.

NFS is also dependent on the underlying hardware and network infrastructure. Performance can be affected by factors such as network latency, bandwidth, and the speed of the storage devices used by the server. To ensure optimal performance, administrators must consider the network setup, ensure that the server hardware is sufficiently powerful, and optimize the configuration of the NFS server and client systems. Tuning various NFS parameters, such as the number of threads or buffer sizes, can help improve performance, but these adjustments require careful monitoring to avoid introducing instability or bottlenecks into the system.

Another challenge is the management of permissions and access control. NFS provides several methods for managing who can access specific files, typically through the use of Access Control Lists (ACLs) or traditional file system permissions. However, because NFS operates across a network, managing these permissions can become more complex, especially in environments where multiple users from different systems need varying levels of access. The traditional UNIX file permission model, based on user, group, and other categories, can sometimes fall short in such scenarios, leading to the adoption of more granular access control mechanisms, such as Kerberos and NFSv4 ACLs.

Despite these challenges, NFS remains a popular and powerful tool for sharing files across a network. Its ease of use, flexibility, and scalability make it an attractive solution for both small and large organizations. In environments where data needs to be accessed by multiple systems,

NFS offers a streamlined and effective way to manage shared resources. As businesses continue to move toward more distributed architectures and cloud-based infrastructures, the role of NFS in enabling seamless file sharing will likely continue to grow. In combination with modern security features and performance tuning, NFS can continue to meet the evolving needs of the IT landscape, making it a vital component of network-based storage solutions.

NFS Server Setup and Configuration

Setting up an NFS server is a fundamental task for enabling file sharing across multiple systems in a network. The process involves configuring the server to share specific directories and then making these directories accessible to clients. The steps for setting up an NFS server can vary slightly depending on the operating system, but the overall procedure remains the same. The first step in configuring an NFS server is installing the necessary NFS server packages. On most Linux distributions, these packages can be easily installed using the package manager. After installation, the server must be configured to share directories with clients, and the correct permissions must be set to ensure secure and reliable access.

Once the NFS server packages are installed, the next step is to configure the directories that will be shared with clients. The server administrator will typically modify the NFS configuration file to define which directories are available for sharing. This configuration file, usually located at /etc/exports, contains a list of directories along with the associated access permissions. The syntax of this file is simple, allowing the administrator to specify the directory path, the host or network allowed to access the directory, and the type of access granted, such as read-only or read-write. It is important to carefully configure this file to ensure that only authorized clients can access the shared directories.

After configuring the /etc/exports file, the NFS server must be restarted for the changes to take effect. Restarting the server ensures that the newly defined shared directories are registered and made available to clients. At this point, the server is ready to share the specified directories, but additional configurations are necessary to control how clients interact with these directories. One important setting to configure is the NFS version to use. While NFSv3 is widely used, NFSv4 offers improved security features and performance enhancements. Depending on the environment, the server administrator may choose to configure the server to use a specific NFS version for compatibility or security reasons.

Access control is a crucial part of configuring an NFS server, and it involves setting up rules to restrict which clients can access shared directories. NFS servers rely on the underlying operating system's user and group management for access control. By default, NFS uses the UID (User ID) and GID (Group ID) of clients to determine access permissions. This means that if a client accesses a directory shared by the NFS server, the server will check the UID and GID of the client against the server's own file system permissions to determine whether the client can read or write to the directory. It is essential for administrators to ensure that the client machines have corresponding UIDs and GIDs to avoid potential permission issues.

In addition to UID and GID-based access control, NFS allows for the use of more advanced security mechanisms, such as Kerberos authentication. Kerberos can be integrated into the NFS server setup to provide a higher level of security by ensuring that both the client and the server authenticate each other before any file operations can take place. This is particularly useful in environments where sensitive data is being shared, and strong authentication is necessary to protect against unauthorized access. Enabling Kerberos authentication requires configuring both the server and the client to use the Kerberos protocol, which adds an additional layer of complexity to the setup but significantly enhances security.

Network configuration is another critical consideration when setting up an NFS server. The server should be configured with a static IP address to ensure that clients can reliably connect to the server using the same address. If the server uses dynamic IP addressing, there is a risk that the IP address may change over time, causing clients to lose access to the server. To prevent this, it is recommended to assign a static IP address to the NFS server, either manually or through a DHCP reservation. This ensures that clients can always reach the server at a known address.

Firewall configuration is another important step in securing an NFS server. NFS uses several network ports for communication, and these ports must be open on the server's firewall to allow clients to connect. In particular, NFS typically uses ports 2049 for NFS traffic, as well as additional ports for portmapper and mountd services. Administrators must ensure that these ports are properly configured on the server's firewall to allow NFS communication while maintaining security. In some cases, it may also be necessary to configure the client firewall to allow inbound connections from the NFS server.

In addition to basic configuration, administrators should consider performance tuning to optimize the NFS server for their specific environment. NFS performance can be affected by various factors, such as network bandwidth, disk I/O performance, and the number of clients accessing the server simultaneously. Tuning parameters such as the number of NFS server threads, the size of the read and write buffers, and the use of asynchronous or synchronous writes can help improve performance. It is also important to monitor the server's resource usage to identify any potential bottlenecks that may affect NFS performance. Tools such as nfsstat and netstat can be useful for monitoring NFS server activity and identifying areas for optimization.

Once the server is properly configured and tuned, it is essential to test the setup to ensure that it is functioning correctly. This can be done by attempting to mount the shared directories on a client machine and verifying that the file system is accessible and that the correct permissions are applied. If any issues arise, the server logs and the client logs can provide valuable information for troubleshooting. Common issues include permission mismatches, network connectivity problems, and incorrect export file configurations. By carefully checking the logs and configuration files, administrators can resolve these issues and ensure that the NFS server is working as expected.

Finally, administrators should consider setting up monitoring and maintenance procedures to ensure the ongoing health and performance of the NFS server. This includes regularly checking the status of the NFS service, reviewing access logs, and updating the server's software to patch any security vulnerabilities. Regular maintenance helps ensure that the NFS server remains secure, stable, and performant as the network and storage requirements evolve over time.

NFS Client Configuration

Configuring an NFS client is a vital step in enabling a machine to access shared file systems from an NFS server. This process ensures that the client can mount remote directories and interact with files as though they are part of the local file system. The process involves several steps, from installing necessary packages to properly configuring the client machine's access to shared directories. Setting up an NFS client requires careful attention to detail to ensure reliable performance, security, and correct permissions between the client and the server.

The first step in configuring an NFS client is ensuring that the necessary NFS client software is installed. On most Linux distributions, the NFS client is available through the package manager, and installing it is as simple as running a command that installs the nfs-common or nfs-utils package. This package includes the essential tools for mounting and managing NFS shares on the client machine. After installation, the client machine is ready to attempt communication with the NFS server, but there are still several additional steps needed to configure the mounting of remote directories.

Once the client machine has the necessary software installed, the next step is to mount the shared directory from the NFS server. This involves identifying the shared directory on the server and choosing a local mount point on the client machine. The mount command is typically used to manually mount the NFS share, specifying the server's address and the directory being shared. For example, the NFS server's IP address or hostname and the export path will be used, followed by the mount point where the directory should be mounted on the client system. The client can then access the files in the remote directory as if they were part of its own local file system.

In addition to manual mounting, it is often desirable to automate the process of mounting NFS shares, particularly in environments where the client machine needs to consistently access the same directories on reboot. To achieve this, administrators can add entries to the /etc/fstab file. This configuration file allows the NFS shares to be automatically mounted at boot time, providing a seamless experience for the user. By adding an entry to the fstab file, the client system will automatically mount the NFS shares upon startup, ensuring that the files are always available without needing manual intervention.

When configuring an NFS client, it is also important to consider the access control and permission settings on the server. The NFS server manages which clients can access its shared directories and with what level of access. This is typically controlled through the server's export configuration file, /etc/exports, which specifies which clients or IP ranges are allowed to access particular directories. The client's user and group IDs (UIDs and GIDs) must match the corresponding IDs on the server to ensure proper access rights. If the client's UID or GID does not correspond to the server's permissions, the client may encounter permission issues when attempting to read or write to the shared directories. It is essential to ensure consistency between the client and server user mappings to avoid these types of errors.

The NFS protocol also supports various mount options that can affect the behavior of the mounted file system. Some of these options can be specified during the mount process or in the /etc/fstab file. For example, administrators can choose to mount the file system as read-only (ro) or read-write (rw), depending on the desired level of access. Other options, such as noexec or nosuid, can be used to enhance security by preventing the execution of binaries or the use of setuid programs on the mounted file system. Mount options can also control performance settings, such as using asynchronous (async) or synchronous (sync) writes, which affect how file writes are handled between the client and server.

For environments requiring secure communication, enabling Kerberos authentication can provide an additional layer of protection between the NFS client and server. Kerberos ensures that both the client and the server authenticate each other before allowing access to the shared files, preventing unauthorized clients from accessing sensitive data.

Configuring Kerberos authentication involves installing the appropriate Kerberos client software on the client machine, configuring the Kerberos server, and ensuring both the client and server are properly synchronized. This setup requires a careful configuration of both the client and server, but it significantly enhances the security of the NFS connection.

Another crucial aspect of NFS client configuration is ensuring proper network connectivity between the client and server. The client machine must be able to resolve the server's hostname or IP address and be able to reach the server over the network. Network issues, such as firewalls or routing misconfigurations, can block NFS traffic and prevent successful communication between the client and the server. To ensure proper network communication, administrators should verify that the NFS server's firewall allows incoming traffic on the appropriate ports, including port 2049 for NFS and additional ports used for other NFS-related services like mountd and rpcbind.

Additionally, administrators must configure the client's firewall to allow outgoing NFS traffic to the server. This includes opening the necessary ports for RPC services and ensuring that any firewall settings on the client machine do not block the communication required for NFS. It is essential to maintain a balance between ensuring proper connectivity and maintaining a secure firewall configuration, as unnecessary open ports can expose the system to potential security risks.

To further improve NFS client performance, administrators can tweak several client-side settings. One of the most important settings is the NFS version used for communication with the server. NFS version 4 offers improvements over earlier versions, including enhanced security and performance features. The client can be configured to specifically request NFSv4, ensuring compatibility with newer NFS servers that support this version. Other performance-related settings, such as the read and write buffer sizes, can be adjusted to optimize the throughput and response time for large file transfers. These settings can be configured during the mount process or added to the /etc/fstab file for persistent changes.

Once the NFS client is configured and the mount is established, it is essential to test the configuration to ensure that everything is functioning correctly. Testing can involve accessing the mounted directories, reading and writing files, and verifying that the client machine can perform file operations without encountering permission or performance issues. If any problems arise, the client and server logs can provide useful diagnostic information for troubleshooting. Log files, such as /var/log/messages or /var/log/syslog, will often indicate issues related to network connectivity, permissions, or mount failures, which can help pinpoint the root cause of the problem.

In addition to basic testing, administrators should also monitor the NFS client's performance and reliability over time. Continuous monitoring of file access patterns, mount status, and server communication can help identify potential issues early and prevent downtime. Tools like nfsstat and netstat can provide useful insights into NFS client activity and network traffic, enabling administrators to fine-tune configurations and maintain optimal performance.

Mounting NFS Shares: Techniques and Best Practices

Mounting NFS shares is a critical task for administrators who need to provide shared access to file systems over a network. It allows clients to access files on remote servers as if they were part of the local file system. The process of mounting NFS shares involves several key steps, and following best practices can ensure that the system is not only functional but also secure and efficient. NFS mounts can be done both manually and automatically, depending on the environment's needs. Regardless of the method chosen, it is important to understand the underlying mechanics of NFS mounting and adhere to best practices to avoid common pitfalls and optimize performance.

To mount an NFS share, the first step is to ensure that the NFS server is properly configured to share specific directories with clients. The server's /etc/exports file controls which directories are shared and specifies the clients that are permitted to access them. Once the server is set up, the client machine needs to mount the shared directory. This can be done with the mount command, specifying the server's IP address or hostname and the shared directory path. Additionally, the client must specify a local mount point where the remote directory will be made available. This allows users on the client machine to access the files as though they are part of the local file system.

One of the most common methods of mounting NFS shares is through the mount command, which can be used manually to mount a specific NFS share to a local directory. For example, using the command "mount -t nfs server:/path/to/share /mnt/localmount" will mount the shared directory from the server to the client's specified local mount point. This method is useful for temporary or ad-hoc mounting, as it allows the client to access the remote files without the need for configuration changes. However, this approach is not ideal for systems that need to access the share consistently, as the mount will not persist after a reboot.

For persistent mounts that survive reboots, the /etc/fstab file is typically used. The fstab file is a configuration file that defines which file systems should be mounted and how they should be mounted during system startup. By adding an entry for the NFS share in the fstab file, administrators can ensure that the share is automatically mounted when the system boots. The fstab entry includes the server's IP address or hostname, the shared directory, the local mount point, and various mount options. This method provides a reliable way to ensure that NFS shares are available to the client at all times without requiring manual intervention after reboot.

One of the key considerations when mounting NFS shares is the use of appropriate mount options. These options control various aspects of how the NFS client interacts with the server, including performance, security, and access control. Some of the most commonly used mount options include read-only (ro), read-write (rw), and noexec. The read-only option ensures that the client can only access the share without modifying its contents, while the read-write option allows both reading and writing. The noexec option prevents the execution of binaries on the mounted file system, which can help mitigate security risks.

For enhanced security, administrators can use additional options such as sec=krb5, which forces the use of Kerberos authentication between the client and server. This ensures that only authorized clients can access the NFS share and provides a stronger level of security for sensitive data. Another important option to consider is the time-to-live (ttl) setting, which controls how long the client will continue trying to reconnect to the server if the connection is lost. Adjusting the ttl value can help ensure that clients do not hang indefinitely when the server is temporarily unavailable.

Another technique that can improve NFS share mounting is the use of automounting. Automounting allows for the automatic mounting of NFS shares when they are accessed, and it can help reduce the need for manual configuration and mount management. This technique is particularly useful in environments with a large number of clients or where shared resources are infrequently used. The automount service is typically configured through the automount configuration files, such as /etc/auto.master and /etc/auto.nfs. These files define the shares to be automatically mounted and their corresponding local mount points. Automounting provides a dynamic approach to NFS sharing, where the system only mounts shares when needed, reducing the load on the system and network when the shares are not in use.

Performance optimization is another important consideration when mounting NFS shares. The performance of NFS can be influenced by factors such as network bandwidth, latency, and the underlying storage performance on the server. To improve performance, administrators can fine-tune the NFS mount options, such as increasing the read and write buffer sizes, adjusting the number of NFS threads, or enabling asynchronous writing (async). These adjustments can help reduce the overhead associated with NFS operations and improve throughput. However, administrators should be cautious when using certain options, such as async, as they can introduce data integrity risks in the event of a system crash or network failure.

In addition to the above techniques, monitoring the NFS shares is essential for maintaining optimal performance and detecting potential issues. Tools such as nfsstat and netstat can provide valuable insights into NFS activity, including the number of requests, response times, and network performance. By regularly monitoring these metrics, administrators can identify potential bottlenecks or performance degradation and take proactive measures to address them. It is also important to monitor the status of the NFS server to ensure that it is running properly and that there are no issues affecting the availability of shared directories.

Access control is another critical aspect of NFS share mounting. By default, NFS relies on UID and GID mappings to determine file access permissions. However, in large or multi-user environments, this can lead to inconsistencies if the client machines have different UID and GID mappings than the server. To address this, administrators can use NFS version 4, which supports more advanced access control mechanisms such as NFSv4 ACLs. These ACLs provide more granular control over which users and groups can access specific files and directories. Additionally, Kerberos authentication can be used to provide strong authentication and ensure that only authorized clients can mount and access the NFS shares.

Properly managing NFS share mounts also involves keeping the system secure. Administrators should ensure that only trusted clients are allowed to access the NFS shares, and this can be done by restricting access through the /etc/exports file on the server. The file should only permit access to specific IP addresses or networks, preventing unauthorized clients from mounting the shares. Additionally, firewalls should be configured to allow NFS traffic while blocking other potentially harmful connections. This layer of security is crucial in protecting sensitive data from unauthorized access.

Regularly updating and maintaining NFS configurations is an important part of ensuring a stable and secure environment. As new versions of NFS and underlying software are released, administrators should review and update the configurations to take advantage of new features, performance improvements, and security patches. Keeping up with best practices for NFS configuration helps prevent issues related to performance, security, and compatibility, ensuring that shared resources remain accessible and secure for all clients.

NFS Security: Authentication and Access Control

Security is a critical aspect of any system that involves sharing files across a network. The Network File System (NFS) is no exception, as it allows clients to access shared directories and files over the network, making it a target for potential security threats. While NFS is a powerful and convenient protocol, it has its vulnerabilities, particularly when it comes to authentication and access control. These vulnerabilities can expose sensitive data to unauthorized users if not properly configured. Therefore, it is essential to implement robust security mechanisms to protect NFS shares and ensure that only authorized clients can access the resources. NFS security primarily revolves around authentication, authorization, and access control, with various strategies available to enhance the protocol's security.

NFS traditionally relied on simple authentication methods based on client IP addresses. When a client connects to the NFS server, the server would check the client's IP address and, if it matched an allowed range, grant access to the shared directories. This approach, while simple, has significant security flaws. An attacker could easily spoof a trusted IP address, gaining unauthorized access to the NFS shares. As a result, NFS's basic IP-based authentication is no longer sufficient for environments where security is a concern.

To address these limitations, NFS has evolved to support stronger authentication methods, such as Kerberos authentication. Kerberos is a network authentication protocol that provides secure authentication for both the client and the server, ensuring that both parties are who they claim to be. By using a trusted third party, called the Key Distribution Center (KDC), Kerberos enables mutual authentication between the client and the server. This means that both the client and the server verify each other's identities before any file operations take place, which greatly reduces the risk of unauthorized access. Kerberos can be integrated into NFSv4, offering a much more secure method of authentication compared to the older methods based solely on IP addresses.

In addition to authentication, access control is a critical element of NFS security. Access control ensures that only authorized users or systems can access specific files or directories on the NFS server. NFS's traditional access control mechanism relied on the UNIX file system's owner, group, and other permissions model. The NFS server would check the UID (user identifier) and GID (group identifier) of the client against the permissions set on the shared directories. However, this method can be problematic, particularly in large environments where UID and GID mappings may not be consistent across systems. For instance, if the UID of a user on the client machine does not match the UID of the same user on the server, the client may be denied access to the shared files, even though the user may have proper access rights on the server.

One way to mitigate this issue is by using NFS version 4 (NFSv4), which introduces more advanced and flexible access control mechanisms. NFSv4 supports Access Control Lists (ACLs), which provide more granular control over file and directory permissions. Unlike the traditional UNIX permissions model, which only distinguishes between owner, group, and others, ACLs allow administrators to define specific permissions for individual users or groups. This enables finer control over who can access shared resources and what actions they can perform. For example, administrators can specify that a particular user can read but not write to a shared directory, or that another user can execute files but not delete them.

In addition to ACLs, NFSv4 also includes support for the use of Kerberos-based access control. When Kerberos authentication is enabled, access to NFS shares can be further restricted based on the user's Kerberos credentials. The Kerberos protocol ensures that only clients with valid authentication tickets can access the resources, and it also allows for the enforcement of more strict access control policies. This integration of Kerberos with NFSv4 greatly enhances the overall security of the system, as it ensures that both authentication and access control are tightly coupled and based on a trusted authentication service.

Another important aspect of NFS security is the management of export options on the server side. The NFS server administrator has the ability to define which clients can access specific shared directories by specifying export options in the /etc/exports file. This file allows administrators to specify the allowed clients by IP address, subnet, or domain name. It is essential to configure this file properly to ensure that only trusted clients can access the shared directories. For example, an administrator can configure the server to allow access only from specific IP addresses or networks, reducing the risk of unauthorized access from untrusted sources.

In addition to restricting access based on IP addresses, the /etc/exports file also allows administrators to specify the level of access granted to each client. For instance, an administrator can grant read-only (ro) access to one client while allowing another client full read-write (rw) access. Furthermore, the file supports options such as no_subtree_check and root_squash, which can help improve security by preventing certain types of attacks. The no_subtree_check option prevents the NFS server from checking the directory tree for every request, which can reduce the attack surface, while root_squash ensures that requests made by the root user on the client are treated as requests by an unprivileged user, thereby preventing potential privilege escalation attacks.

It is also essential to secure the network traffic between the NFS client and server. By default, NFS does not encrypt its traffic, meaning that data transferred between the client and the server can be intercepted by malicious actors on the network. This is especially concerning when NFS is used over untrusted networks, such as the internet. To mitigate this risk, administrators can use secure tunneling protocols like VPNs or SSH to encrypt NFS traffic. Another option is to enable Transport Layer Security (TLS) for NFSv4, which provides encryption for both the data and the communication channels between the client and server. Enabling TLS ensures that the data being transferred is protected from eavesdropping and tampering, adding an additional layer of security.

To further enhance security, NFS servers should be carefully monitored for unauthorized access attempts. Regularly checking the server logs for suspicious activity, such as failed authentication attempts or unusual access patterns, can help detect potential security breaches early. Additionally, security tools such as intrusion detection systems (IDS) can be deployed to monitor the NFS server and alert administrators to any suspicious activity. Regular updates to the NFS server software and the underlying operating system are also essential for maintaining a secure environment, as vulnerabilities in older versions of the software can be exploited by attackers.

Properly configuring and maintaining NFS security requires careful planning and attention to detail. By implementing strong authentication methods like Kerberos, using advanced access control mechanisms like NFSv4 ACLs, and properly securing network traffic, administrators can significantly reduce the risk of unauthorized access to shared resources. These measures, combined with best practices for server configuration and monitoring, ensure that NFS can be used securely in environments of all sizes, from small businesses to large enterprise networks.

NFS Performance Optimization

NFS (Network File System) is an essential tool for sharing files across a network, but its performance can be significantly influenced by various factors such as network conditions, server load, and client configurations. Optimizing NFS performance is crucial for ensuring that file access is efficient, reliable, and responsive. This task involves adjusting server and client settings, tweaking network configurations, and considering factors like workload distribution, hardware resources, and protocol versions. Each of these elements plays a role in the overall performance of an NFS system, and a comprehensive approach is required to maximize its efficiency.

One of the first steps in optimizing NFS performance is configuring the server's hardware and software appropriately. The server's CPU, memory, and disk I/O capabilities must be sufficient to handle the expected load, especially in environments with high traffic or large datasets. For instance, servers with faster processors and more memory are better equipped to handle multiple NFS requests simultaneously, which can lead to improved response times. Additionally, using high-performance storage devices, such as SSDs (Solid State Drives), can provide faster data access compared to traditional hard drives, which helps reduce latency when serving large files over the network.

In terms of software, the NFS server should be running the latest stable version of the NFS protocol. NFSv4, for example, offers improvements in performance over previous versions, including better caching mechanisms and more efficient handling of file operations. Upgrading to the latest version ensures that the server can take advantage of these enhancements. Along with the version of NFS, the server configuration must also be optimized. Parameters such as the number of NFS server threads, buffer sizes, and the use of asynchronous versus synchronous writes can be fine-tuned to improve performance. Asynchronous writes, for instance, can improve throughput by allowing the server to process other requests while waiting for disk operations to complete, though this option should be used cautiously as it can increase the risk of data corruption during power failures or system crashes.

Network performance is another critical factor that directly impacts NFS performance. A fast and reliable network connection between the server and clients is essential for minimizing delays and ensuring efficient data transfer. The bandwidth and latency of the network link will influence the overall speed of file operations. To optimize network performance, administrators can ensure that the NFS server and clients are connected via high-speed Ethernet or fiber-optic links, especially in environments with large file transfers or multiple clients accessing the server concurrently. It is also important to minimize network congestion and ensure that network interfaces are not overloaded with excessive traffic. Using dedicated networks for NFS traffic or implementing VLANs (Virtual Local Area Networks) to separate NFS traffic from other types of network traffic can help ensure that NFS traffic has enough bandwidth to operate smoothly.

Optimizing the NFS client configuration is equally important. The NFS client settings, such as the read and write buffer sizes, can have a significant effect on the performance of file transfers. By increasing the buffer sizes, the client can handle larger chunks of data, reducing the number of network round trips required for file operations. This is particularly beneficial for high-throughput environments, where transferring large files or many small files is common. Adjusting the client's NFS protocol version is also an essential consideration. NFSv4 offers improved performance compared to earlier versions by reducing the number of network operations required for certain tasks, as well as providing better handling of file locking and state management. If both the client and server support NFSv4, using this version is recommended for better performance.

The NFS cache settings are another crucial area to address when optimizing performance. NFS uses caching to improve performance by storing frequently accessed data in memory, which reduces the need to repeatedly fetch data from disk. However, improper cache configurations can lead to inconsistent or outdated data being served to clients. Fine-tuning cache parameters can help ensure that the data being accessed is up to date while maintaining optimal performance. On the server side, administrators can adjust the number of cache entries and the cache timeout settings to balance performance and data consistency. On the client side, cache settings can be adjusted to control the amount of data stored locally and the duration of time that cached data remains valid. Increasing the cache size can improve performance by reducing the need for repeated network requests, but it must be balanced with the need for fresh data and the available memory on the client machine.

Load balancing is another effective technique for optimizing NFS performance in environments with multiple clients or high traffic. By distributing the NFS workload across multiple servers or storage devices, administrators can reduce the load on a single server and improve overall throughput. Load balancing can be achieved through various methods, such as using round-robin DNS to direct clients to different NFS servers or implementing hardware-based load balancers to manage the distribution of NFS requests. In large-scale environments, using a distributed file system or storage solution, such as a clustered NFS setup, can help ensure that NFS services are available and performant even under heavy demand.

Another optimization technique involves using NFS over a high-performance transport protocol. While NFS typically runs over UDP (User Datagram Protocol) or TCP (Transmission Control Protocol), the choice of protocol can affect performance depending on the network environment. UDP can provide lower latency for some applications, but it is less reliable than TCP and may result in data loss in case of network issues. TCP, on the other hand, is more reliable and ensures data integrity, but it may introduce slightly higher overhead due to its error-checking mechanisms. In environments where reliability is more critical than low latency, using TCP is generally recommended for NFS. Additionally, enabling NFS's TCP options, such as large read and write buffer sizes, can improve throughput by reducing the number of retransmissions required during file transfers.

The use of Jumbo Frames is another network optimization technique that can improve NFS performance. Jumbo Frames allow larger packets to be transmitted over the network, reducing the overhead associated with sending multiple smaller packets. This is particularly beneficial in high-throughput environments where large files are being transferred, as it reduces the number of network transactions required to move data. To take full advantage of Jumbo Frames, both the server and the client must support this feature, and the network infrastructure must be configured to handle larger frame sizes.

In high-demand environments, it is essential to monitor and analyze NFS performance regularly. Using tools like nfsstat, iostat, and netstat can provide valuable insights into the performance of the NFS system. These tools can help identify bottlenecks in the system, such as high disk I/O wait times or network congestion, and allow administrators to address performance issues proactively. By analyzing performance metrics over time, administrators can identify trends and adjust configurations as needed to maintain optimal performance.

Ultimately, optimizing NFS performance requires a holistic approach that takes into account the hardware, network, server and client configurations, and workload characteristics. By tuning the various parameters associated with NFS, ensuring that the underlying infrastructure is capable of handling the expected load, and regularly monitoring the system for potential bottlenecks, administrators can ensure that NFS provides the performance necessary to support modern distributed environments.

Troubleshooting NFS Connections

When working with NFS (Network File System) connections, issues can arise that prevent clients from accessing shared directories or cause performance degradation. These problems can range from simple misconfigurations to complex network issues. Troubleshooting NFS connections requires a systematic approach to identify the root cause of the problem, whether it is related to server settings, client configurations, network connectivity, or other factors. By using a combination of diagnostic tools, log analysis, and common troubleshooting steps, administrators can resolve NFS issues and ensure smooth operation of file-sharing services.

The first step in troubleshooting an NFS connection is to confirm that both the NFS server and the client are running properly. The server should be up and operational, and the NFS service should be actively listening for client requests. On the server side, administrators can use tools like systemctl or service to verify that the NFS service is running. In some cases, the NFS server may fail to start or may crash due to configuration issues, missing dependencies, or resource constraints. Checking the server's status with system logs can provide insight into whether the service is encountering errors that need to be addressed.

On the client side, ensuring that the NFS client is properly installed and configured is essential. The client machine should have the appropriate NFS client software installed, which can be verified using package management tools like apt or yum on Linux-based systems. If the software is missing or incorrectly installed, the client will not be able to communicate with the NFS server. Additionally, verifying that the client is attempting to mount the correct NFS share and using the appropriate mount options is crucial for successful communication.

One of the most common issues when troubleshooting NFS connections is ensuring proper network connectivity between the client and server. NFS relies on network communication to function, and if the client cannot reach the server due to network misconfigurations or hardware issues, it will not be able to mount the shared directories. Checking the network connection involves ensuring that both machines are on the same network or that proper routing is in place. Administrators should verify that the server and client can ping each other using their IP addresses or hostnames to confirm that there are no connectivity issues. If pinging fails, troubleshooting the network infrastructure, including routers, switches, and firewalls, is necessary to ensure that NFS traffic is not being blocked.

If the client and server can communicate over the network but NFS shares are still inaccessible, the next step is to check the server's export configuration. The server's /etc/exports file defines which directories are shared with clients and the specific access permissions. If the file is misconfigured or the client's IP address is not listed, the client will be unable to access the shared directories. Common errors in this file include incorrect file paths, missing client IP addresses, or improper access control options. Verifying the contents of the /etc/exports file and ensuring that the correct directories are shared with the appropriate clients can often resolve these types of issues.

Another potential issue involves file and directory permissions on the NFS server. Since NFS relies on UNIX-style file permissions (UIDs and GIDs) to control access, mismatches between the client and server's user and group IDs can lead to permission denials. If the client and server are using different user and group IDs for the same users, the client may not have the necessary permissions to read or write to the shared directories. This issue can be particularly problematic in environments with multiple clients or in cases where the server and client systems have different user management schemes. To resolve this, administrators can ensure that the same UIDs and GIDs are used across all systems or implement a centralized authentication system like NIS or LDAP to synchronize user and group information.

NFS version mismatches can also cause issues, particularly if the client and server are using different versions of the NFS protocol. For example, NFSv3 and NFSv4 are not fully compatible, and using the wrong version can lead to failures in mounting shares. Ensuring that both the client and server are configured to use the same NFS version is essential for successful communication. Administrators can specify the NFS version when mounting shares on the client side using the -o nfsvers=X option, where X is the version number. In environments that support NFSv4, it is recommended to use this version due to its enhanced security features and improved performance over older versions.

Another common problem that may arise in NFS configurations is related to the NFS lock manager. NFS uses a locking mechanism to prevent multiple clients from making conflicting changes to the same file simultaneously. If the lock manager is not functioning properly, clients may experience issues such as being unable to access files or directories, or file operations may fail unexpectedly. To troubleshoot lock manager issues, administrators should check whether the rpc.lockd service is running on both the client and server. If this service is not running, NFS clients may be unable to obtain file locks, leading to inconsistencies and errors.

Firewall settings on both the client and server can also interfere with NFS connections. NFS uses a range of ports for communication, including port 2049 for NFS itself, as well as additional ports for related services such as rpcbind and mountd. If a firewall is blocking these ports, clients will not be able to access the NFS server. Checking firewall configurations on both the client and server sides to ensure that the necessary ports are open is crucial for resolving connection issues. Administrators should also verify that any intermediate firewalls, such as those in routers or security appliances, are not blocking NFS traffic.

Another tool that can be useful when troubleshooting NFS connections is nfsstat. This command provides detailed statistics on NFS client and server performance, including information on operations, errors, and network activity. By analyzing the output of nfsstat, administrators can identify common issues such as high response times, excessive retransmissions, or failed operations. Similarly, the rpcinfo command can be used to check the status of RPC services on the server and verify that the required services are available for NFS communication.

Log files on both the client and server can provide valuable information when diagnosing NFS issues. Server logs, typically located in /var/log/messages or /var/log/syslog, can reveal errors related to NFS services, client connections, and file operations. On the client side, the dmesg command can be used to check for any kernel-level errors or warnings related to NFS. Analyzing these logs can help identify the specific error that is preventing the NFS connection from working properly.

By systematically verifying network connectivity, server configurations, file permissions, protocol versions, and firewall settings, administrators can quickly identify and resolve NFS connection issues. While the troubleshooting process can be complex, using the right tools and techniques can significantly reduce the time required to restore proper NFS functionality. Understanding the root cause of NFS connection problems is essential for maintaining a stable and efficient file-sharing environment.

NFS Versions: v3 vs v4 vs v4.1

The Network File System (NFS) has undergone significant evolution since its inception, with each new version bringing improvements in performance, security, and scalability. NFS versions 3, 4, and 4.1 are widely used, and understanding their differences is crucial for administrators to make informed decisions about which version to use in their environment. While NFSv3 has been a reliable workhorse for many years, NFSv4 and its subsequent release, NFSv4.1, have introduced a range of features designed to address the evolving needs of modern networked file systems. Each version comes with its own set of strengths, limitations, and use cases, and understanding how they differ can help in selecting the right version for specific requirements.

NFSv3 was introduced in 1995 and remains one of the most widely used versions of NFS due to its simplicity and stability. It operates over both UDP and TCP, though in modern networks, TCP is often preferred for its reliability. One of the main advantages of NFSv3 is its stateless nature, which means that each request is independent and does not require the server to maintain any information about the client's previous interactions. This statelessness makes NFSv3 highly resilient in environments where reliability is essential, as clients can reconnect to the server without needing to worry about session states. However, the lack of state information also means that NFSv3 does not support advanced features like file locking in a robust way, which can lead to issues when multiple clients attempt to modify the same file simultaneously.

Despite its widespread use, NFSv3 has several limitations, particularly in the areas of security and performance. NFSv3 does not provide built-in encryption or strong authentication mechanisms, making it vulnerable to security risks such as man-in-the-middle attacks and unauthorized access. The protocol also lacks support for more advanced file access control features, such as fine-grained access control lists (ACLs), which are increasingly necessary in modern, distributed environments. Additionally, while NFSv3 performs well in many situations, its lack of support for features such as caching and stateful operations limits its ability to scale efficiently in large, complex networks with many clients.

NFSv4 was introduced in 2000 as a major overhaul of the protocol, addressing many of the limitations of NFSv3. One of the most significant changes in NFSv4 is the introduction of statefulness. Unlike NFSv3, NFSv4 maintains session information between the client and the server, allowing for more efficient operations and better handling of concurrent file accesses. This stateful nature enables NFSv4 to support more advanced features like file locking, delegation, and compound operations. File locking in particular is much more reliable in NFSv4, allowing multiple clients to work on the same file without conflicting with each other. These features make NFSv4 far more suitable for modern workloads, particularly in environments where multiple users or applications need to access and modify files simultaneously.

Another significant improvement in NFSv4 is the introduction of a more robust security model. NFSv4 includes support for Kerberos-based authentication, which provides strong encryption and authentication for both the client and server. This eliminates many of the security vulnerabilities present in NFSv3, making NFSv4 a more secure option for environments where data integrity and confidentiality are critical. Additionally, NFSv4 supports the use of access control lists (ACLs), which provide more granular control over file and directory permissions. ACLs allow administrators to define specific permissions for individual users and groups, enhancing security in multi-user environments where fine-grained access control is needed.

NFSv4 also improved performance through better handling of large numbers of requests and enhanced caching mechanisms. For example, it introduced support for compound operations, which allow multiple file system operations to be bundled into a single request. This reduces the overhead of making multiple round-trip calls between the client and server, improving efficiency and reducing latency. NFSv4 also offers better support for modern file systems and storage solutions, making it a more scalable option for large-scale environments.

However, despite these improvements, NFSv4 also comes with its own set of challenges. One of the most significant drawbacks of NFSv4 is its complexity. The stateful nature of the protocol requires more sophisticated server and client configurations, and administrators may find the setup and management of NFSv4 to be more involved than NFSv3. Additionally, while NFSv4 has better support for security, it may require additional configuration steps, such as setting up Kerberos authentication, which can be complex in some environments.

NFSv4.1, released in 2010, introduced several important enhancements over NFSv4, particularly in terms of performance and scalability. One of the key features of NFSv4.1 is the introduction of parallel NFS (pNFS), which enables the distribution of file data across multiple storage devices. This allows for greater scalability and improved performance in environments with high throughput or large data sets. With pNFS, clients can directly access multiple storage devices simultaneously, reducing bottlenecks and improving the efficiency of file access operations.

Another notable improvement in NFSv4.1 is the introduction of session trunking, which allows multiple network connections between the client and server. This enhances fault tolerance and improves performance by distributing the load across multiple connections. If one connection fails, the client can switch to another connection without disrupting file access, making NFSv4.1 more resilient to network failures and providing better overall reliability in high-availability environments.

In addition to these performance improvements, NFSv4.1 also includes better support for complex environments with multiple clients. It introduces enhanced delegation mechanisms, allowing clients to cache file data more efficiently and reducing the number of requests that need to be made to the server. This reduces latency and improves performance, particularly in environments where files are frequently accessed and modified by multiple clients.

Despite these advantages, NFSv4.1 still inherits many of the complexities of NFSv4. The additional features introduced in NFSv4.1 require more careful configuration and tuning to achieve optimal performance. As with NFSv4, administrators must also deal with the complexity of session management and the need for secure authentication, such as Kerberos. Furthermore, while pNFS can greatly improve scalability in large environments, it requires a compatible storage backend, which may not always be available in older or legacy systems.

In summary, NFSv3, NFSv4, and NFSv4.1 each have their own strengths and weaknesses. NFSv3 remains a reliable choice for simpler environments with fewer security concerns and less need for advanced features. NFSv4 is the preferred choice for modern, secure, and stateful environments, offering improved security and performance. NFSv4.1 builds upon NFSv4 by introducing additional performance enhancements, particularly in large-scale environments, but at the cost of increased complexity. By understanding the differences between these versions, administrators can make informed decisions about which version is best suited for their specific use case, balancing performance, security, and scalability requirements.

NFS Export Options and Customization

The ability to configure export options in NFS (Network File System) allows system administrators to fine-tune how directories are shared between NFS servers and clients. Export options are defined in the server's /etc/exports file, where administrators specify the directories they wish to share and the access controls for each shared directory. These options provide flexibility in managing permissions, controlling access, and optimizing performance based on specific needs. Understanding how to properly configure and customize these export options is essential for maintaining a secure, efficient, and well-performing NFS environment.

When configuring export options, the most fundamental task is specifying which directories are to be shared and which clients or networks are permitted to access them. The /etc/exports file contains entries that follow a specific format, where the directory to be shared is listed alongside the host or network allowed to mount it. The basic syntax for an export entry includes the path of the shared directory, followed by the allowed client's IP address or network, and then the export options. For example, if an administrator wanted to share the /data directory with a specific client, the entry might look like /data client_ip_address(rw,sync,no_subtree_check).

Export options define the level of access that a client has to the shared directory. One of the most important options is read-write (rw) or read-only (ro). The read-write option allows clients to modify files on the shared directory, while read-only restricts them to viewing the files without making changes. This distinction is crucial when sharing sensitive data, as limiting access to read-only prevents unintended modifications. In environments where clients require full access to files for tasks such as backups or data processing, the rw option is appropriate. However, for situations where data integrity must be preserved or where unauthorized changes need to be prevented, the ro option is preferred.

Another key option to consider is the no_subtree_check option. By default, NFS performs a check to ensure that the client is requesting a file within the shared directory's subtree. If this option is enabled, NFS verifies that the requested file or directory is within the root directory being exported. However, enabling no_subtree_check can improve performance in certain environments by skipping this check, which reduces the overhead of file lookups. It is especially beneficial in large file systems or when the directory structure is complex. While this option can provide performance gains, it can also introduce risks, as it allows clients to access subdirectories or files outside the intended boundaries if their paths are incorrectly specified.

The root_squash option is another important security feature. It is used to prevent the root user on the client machine from having root access to the NFS server's shared directories. When root_squash is enabled, any requests from the root user on the client machine are mapped to the anonymous user or a specified non-privileged user on the server. This option helps prevent potential security breaches that could occur if a malicious user gained root access on the client machine, as it limits the privileges granted to the root user in the shared directory. For environments where administrative privileges must be tightly controlled, enabling root_squash provides an additional layer of protection against unauthorized access.

To fine-tune the security of NFS exports, administrators can also use the no_all_squash option. This option is the inverse of root_squash and allows the root user on the client machine to have root access to the NFS server's shared directory. While this may be necessary in certain administrative scenarios, it should be used with caution, as it grants the client's root user full control over the exported directory. In most cases, administrators prefer to use root_squash to limit the access of client root users and reduce the risk of security vulnerabilities.

The secure and insecure options control the type of connection allowed between the NFS server and client. By default, NFS allows connections only from clients that are using ports lower than 1024, considered "secure." However, some clients may need to use higher ports for specific applications or configurations. In this case, the insecure option can be enabled, allowing the NFS server to accept connections from clients using any port. While this option may be necessary in certain circumstances, it should be used carefully, as it can expose the server to potential security risks by allowing connections from higher-numbered ports that may not be properly validated.

The sync and async options control how file writes are handled by the NFS server. The sync option ensures that the server acknowledges the client's write request only after the data has been committed to disk. This guarantees data integrity, as it ensures that no data is lost in the event of a server crash or power failure. However, the sync option can lead to higher latency and slower write operations, as each write request must be completed before the server responds. In contrast, the async option allows the server to respond to the client's write request without waiting for the data to be written to disk. This improves performance by reducing latency but introduces the risk of data loss if the server crashes before the data is written. The choice between sync and async depends on the specific needs of the environment. For mission-critical applications where data integrity is paramount, sync is recommended. However, for environments where performance is more important, and data loss is less of a concern, async may be acceptable.

The access control features of NFS can also be customized with additional options such as no_root_squash, which allows the root user on the server to have root-level access to the exported directory. This option can be beneficial in environments where users require root-level access on the NFS client. However, enabling this option can introduce a security risk, so it should be used sparingly and with caution.

In large-scale or distributed environments, administrators may need to export directories to multiple clients or networks. The /etc/exports file allows for a variety of advanced configurations to achieve this. For example, administrators can specify different export options for different clients or subnets. This provides the flexibility to grant different levels of access or control to different groups of clients. In multi-host environments, it is also possible to configure the NFS server to allow certain clients to mount specific subdirectories while preventing others from accessing sensitive or confidential data stored on the same server.

Monitoring NFS export performance and usage is another aspect of customization. Administrators can use tools such as nfsstat, rpcinfo, and showmount to monitor NFS export statistics, check the status of the NFS server, and ensure that shares are being accessed as expected. These tools can help identify performance bottlenecks, detect unauthorized access attempts, and provide valuable insights into how the NFS server is being utilized. Regular monitoring ensures that the NFS configuration remains optimal, secure, and efficient.

Properly configuring and customizing NFS export options requires a thorough understanding of the available options and how they affect security, performance, and accessibility. Administrators should carefully consider the needs of their specific environment, balancing the need for performance with the importance of security. By properly configuring export options, system administrators can ensure that NFS provides a secure, reliable, and high-performance file-sharing solution.

Automating NFS Mounts with fstab

In a networked environment where multiple clients need to access shared directories from an NFS (Network File System) server, automating the process of mounting these directories is essential for efficiency and reliability. One of the most effective ways to achieve this is by using the /etc/fstab file, a configuration file that contains information about file systems and their mounting options. The fstab file allows system administrators to automate the mounting of NFS shares at boot time, ensuring that the necessary network file systems are always available when the system starts. This is especially useful in environments with multiple clients, as it reduces the need for manual intervention and ensures that file access is consistently available across all machines.

The /etc/fstab file is a fundamental component of Linux and Unix-like operating systems. It defines the relationship between file systems and their respective mount points, indicating how and where each file system should be mounted. The file contains a list of entries, with each entry corresponding to a specific file system or partition. For NFS mounts, the fstab file allows administrators to define which remote NFS shares should be mounted, as well as the mount options required for accessing these shares. These options specify whether the mount should be read-only or read-write, how the system should handle file locking, and other parameters that influence performance and security.

To automate an NFS mount, the administrator must first edit the /etc/fstab file and add a new entry for the NFS share. The basic format for an NFS mount entry in fstab consists of the following components: the remote NFS server's address and the shared directory path, the local mount point on the client system, the file system type (in this case, nfs), and the mount options. For example, an entry in the fstab file might look like this: server:/path/to/share /mnt/nfs nfs defaults o o. This tells the system to mount the NFS share located at /path/to/share on the NFS server, placing it at the local mount point /mnt/nfs on the client machine. The nfs designation specifies that the file system is an NFS share, and the defaults option applies default settings to the mount.

Once the entry has been added to the fstab file, the NFS share will be mounted automatically the next time the system is rebooted. The mount command can also be used to mount the shares immediately without rebooting by running mount -a, which reads the fstab file and mounts all file systems listed within it. This is particularly useful for testing the configuration before rebooting the system to ensure that the NFS shares are mounted correctly.

While the default mount options may be sufficient for many environments, there are various options that administrators can use to customize the NFS mount behavior to better suit their needs. These options can be specified in the fstab entry after the file system type. For example, the rw option grants read-write access to the NFS share, allowing clients to modify files, while the ro option mounts the share as read-only, preventing any changes to the shared data. If security is a concern, administrators can use the sec option to specify an authentication method, such as sec=krb5 for Kerberos authentication, to ensure that only authenticated clients can mount the share.

Another important option to consider when automating NFS mounts is the timeo option, which specifies the time in seconds that the client should wait before retrying a request to the NFS server. By adjusting the timeo value, administrators can control how aggressively the client retries failed connections, which can be useful in environments with intermittent network connectivity or high server load. The rsize and wsize options control the size of the read and write buffers used during data transfer, and increasing these values can improve performance in environments with high throughput requirements. However, administrators must be careful not to set these values too high, as doing so can lead to network congestion or other issues.

NFS clients can also specify the bg (background) option in the fstab file, which allows the mount to proceed in the background if the server is unreachable. This can be useful in environments where network connectivity is unreliable, as it ensures that the system can still boot even if the NFS server is temporarily unavailable. Additionally, the noauto option can be used to prevent the NFS mount from being automatically mounted at boot time. This can be useful in situations where the administrator wants to manually mount the NFS share later or only mount it under specific conditions.

One of the advantages of using fstab to automate NFS mounts is that it ensures consistent behavior across all systems. Once the entry has been configured, every client that uses the same fstab file will mount the NFS share in the same way, with the same options and mount points. This simplifies system administration in environments with multiple clients, as there is no need to configure each system individually. The fstab file can be shared among systems, ensuring that all clients access the same NFS shares in a consistent manner, which is essential for collaborative work and data management.

However, there are some potential pitfalls to be aware of when automating NFS mounts using fstab. For example, if the NFS server is unavailable during boot time, the system may hang while attempting to mount the shares. To mitigate this risk, administrators can use the soft option in the fstab entry, which causes the client to fail the mount operation if the NFS server is unreachable, rather than hanging indefinitely. While this option ensures that the system will not be delayed, it can also result in data loss or corruption if the client is actively writing to the NFS share at the time of failure. In such cases, the hard option may be preferred, as it ensures that the client will retry indefinitely until the server becomes available, providing more robust protection for critical data.

Another potential issue is related to network performance. NFS relies heavily on network connectivity, and poor network performance can result in slow file operations, increased latency, or even failures to mount the NFS share. To optimize NFS performance, administrators can use a variety of network tuning parameters in the fstab file, such as adjusting the TCP buffer size or enabling the async option to allow the client to complete write operations more quickly. These adjustments can improve the overall performance of NFS mounts but must be used with care to avoid compromising data integrity.

When configuring automated NFS mounts, it is also important to consider the network environment and ensure that the NFS server is properly secured. NFS shares should be restricted to trusted clients, and the fstab file should only contain entries for known and authorized servers. Administrators can use firewall rules or network segmentation to further protect the NFS server from unauthorized access. Additionally, advanced options such as Kerberos authentication can be specified in the fstab file to ensure secure communication between the client and server.

Automating NFS mounts with fstab simplifies the management of NFS shares across multiple clients and ensures that necessary file systems are available at boot time. By customizing the mount options, administrators can optimize performance, enhance security, and tailor the behavior of NFS mounts to suit the specific needs of the environment. The fstab file provides a powerful and flexible way to manage NFS mounts, making it an essential tool for system administrators working with networked file systems.

Using NFS in Distributed File Systems

Network File System (NFS) has long been an essential protocol for sharing files across networks, providing a transparent and easy-to-use mechanism for accessing remote directories. As distributed systems have become more prevalent, the role of NFS in facilitating communication between distributed file systems has grown significantly. A distributed file system (DFS) allows multiple machines, often in different locations, to share files and directories over a network, providing users and applications with the ability to access and modify data as if it were stored locally. NFS plays a crucial part in such systems by enabling the efficient sharing of file systems across distributed environments, facilitating collaboration, and ensuring that all clients can access and update files seamlessly.

In a distributed file system setup, NFS allows clients to mount directories located on remote servers as if they were part of their local file system. This ability to mount remote directories enables centralized management of files, simplifying backup, recovery, and security management. By using NFS in a distributed environment, organizations can reduce the complexity of file storage management, minimize redundancy, and ensure data consistency across multiple machines. With the rise of cloud computing and high-performance computing environments, NFS has adapted to meet the demands of modern distributed file systems, providing solutions for managing large datasets, enhancing scalability, and supporting a wide range of applications.

The basic operation of NFS in a distributed system involves a client-server model, where the client requests access to files located on the server. The NFS protocol facilitates the transfer of data over the network, allowing clients to interact with remote files as though they were local. NFS can work over different transport protocols, with TCP being the preferred choice for most modern systems due to its reliability and error-checking features. By allowing remote file systems to be mounted on local machines, NFS enables users to access shared resources and interact with data without needing to know the specifics of where or how the files are stored.

One of the significant advantages of using NFS in distributed file systems is its transparency. When configured properly, users and applications accessing files over NFS do not need to be aware that the files are stored remotely. They interact with the files as though they were stored locally on their machines. This is particularly useful in collaborative environments where multiple users may be working on the same data set, as NFS ensures that changes made by one user are immediately visible to others. The transparency provided by NFS is essential for maintaining smooth workflows in large-scale distributed systems, where data is spread across multiple servers and locations.

NFS also helps in optimizing storage in distributed environments. By centralizing data storage on a few servers, organizations can streamline data management and reduce the overhead associated with maintaining local copies of files on each machine. This reduces storage costs, simplifies backup processes, and enables easier data replication across the distributed file system. However, centralization comes with its own set of challenges, particularly in terms of scalability and performance. As the number of clients grows or the amount of data being accessed increases, NFS may encounter bottlenecks that affect performance. These performance issues can arise due to network congestion, high server load, or limitations in the server's hardware.

To address these performance concerns, NFS can be optimized in several ways. The use of faster network infrastructure, such as gigabit or fiber-optic connections, can alleviate some of the strain caused by network latency. In addition, administrators can tweak various NFS parameters, such as read and write buffer sizes, to improve throughput. The use of NFS version 4 and NFS version 4.1, which includes optimizations for performance and security, can also help address some of these challenges. NFSv4 introduces features such as compound operations, which allow multiple file operations to be bundled into a single request, reducing the number of round-trip communications between the client and server. This not only improves performance but also reduces the load on the network and the server.

Another critical consideration when using NFS in distributed file systems is security. By default, NFS does not provide encryption for the data being transferred between the client and the server, which can pose significant risks in untrusted networks. In a distributed file system, where data might traverse multiple network segments, this lack of encryption can expose sensitive information to eavesdropping or tampering. To address these security concerns, organizations can implement solutions such as Virtual Private Networks (VPNs) or Secure Socket Layer (SSL) tunneling to encrypt the NFS traffic. Additionally, enabling Kerberos authentication in NFSv4 provides an extra layer of security, ensuring that both the client and the server authenticate each other before any data is exchanged.

The scalability of NFS is another factor to consider when using it in distributed file systems. As the number of clients increases, the NFS server can become a potential bottleneck. In large-scale distributed environments, it may be necessary to deploy multiple NFS servers to distribute the load and improve performance. This can be achieved by using techniques such as load balancing and clustering. In a clustered NFS setup, multiple NFS servers work together to handle client requests, providing redundancy and improving scalability. By distributing the load across multiple servers, administrators can ensure that the system can handle a growing number of clients and increasing data access demands.

One of the main challenges in using NFS in distributed file systems is managing file consistency. In environments where multiple clients are accessing and modifying the same files simultaneously, it is essential to ensure that the changes made by one client are immediately visible to others. NFSv4 addresses some of these issues by introducing stronger file locking mechanisms, which allow clients to lock files or portions of files to prevent simultaneous conflicting changes. While these locking mechanisms are an improvement over earlier versions of NFS, they may not be sufficient in all situations. In highly concurrent environments, additional mechanisms, such as distributed caching or data replication, may be necessary to ensure consistency and prevent data corruption.

The use of NFS in distributed file systems also requires careful management of network resources. NFS can put a significant load on the network, especially in environments where large files are being transferred or accessed by many clients simultaneously. This can lead to congestion and slow performance if the network infrastructure is not adequately designed to handle the increased traffic. To address this, administrators can use Quality of Service (QoS) techniques to prioritize NFS traffic and ensure that it receives the necessary bandwidth. Additionally, network monitoring tools can help administrators track performance metrics and identify potential bottlenecks in the network or on the server.

In summary, NFS is a powerful tool for enabling file sharing in distributed file systems, offering transparency, scalability, and ease of management. However, as with any technology, there are challenges associated with its use in large-scale or complex distributed environments. By optimizing NFS for performance, implementing strong security measures, and ensuring proper network configuration, organizations can take full advantage of NFS's capabilities while mitigating potential risks.

NFS vs SMB: Comparison and Use Cases

Network File System (NFS) and Server Message Block (SMB) are two of the most widely used protocols for sharing files across networks. Both protocols enable systems to share files and allow users to access those files from remote machines. However, they differ significantly in terms of their origins, underlying technology, performance, and specific use cases. Understanding the differences between NFS and SMB is essential for choosing the right protocol based on the needs of an organization or a specific network environment. Both protocols have evolved over time and are tailored to different use cases, making it important to evaluate the strengths and limitations of each when designing a network file sharing solution.

NFS, originally developed in the 1980s by Sun Microsystems, is a protocol designed primarily for UNIX-like operating systems, including Linux, FreeBSD, and macOS. NFS allows machines to mount remote directories and access them as if they were part of the local file system. The protocol operates on a client-server model, where the NFS server shares directories, and clients can mount and access those directories over a network. One of the key features of NFS is its transparency; users and applications interact with files stored on remote servers in much the same way they would interact with local files. This makes it an attractive option in environments where UNIX-based systems are prevalent and file sharing is needed across multiple systems.

On the other hand, SMB is a network file sharing protocol that originated with Microsoft in the 1980s. SMB is commonly used in Windows environments, though it is also supported on other operating systems through software implementations such as Samba. Like NFS, SMB allows for file sharing between computers, but it is designed with Windows clients in mind and provides a richer set of features for managing shared files. SMB operates on a more complex client-server architecture compared to NFS and includes features such as file locking, network browsing, and access control. In addition to file sharing, SMB is also used for other types of network communication, such as printer sharing and inter-process communication.

One of the main differences between NFS and SMB is their underlying protocol architecture. NFS uses the stateless model, which means that the server does not maintain session information between client requests. Each NFS request is treated independently, making it more resilient to network failures. In contrast, SMB uses a stateful model, where the server maintains session information and is responsible for managing the connections with clients. This allows SMB to support more advanced features such as file locking, but it also means that if a connection is interrupted, the client must re-establish the session. In environments where reliability is paramount, NFS's statelessness can be an advantage as it allows clients to reconnect without losing access to shared resources.

Another significant difference between NFS and SMB is the way they handle authentication and security. NFS, particularly in its earlier versions, was designed without a strong focus on security. While newer versions, such as NFSv4, have introduced support for Kerberos authentication and encryption, NFS is still often seen as less secure than SMB. SMB, on the other hand, has evolved significantly in terms of security. With the introduction of SMB2 and SMB3, Microsoft included stronger encryption, signing, and authentication mechanisms, making SMB a more secure choice for file sharing. SMB can also integrate with Active Directory, enabling fine-grained control over user authentication and access management, which is particularly beneficial in Windows-based environments where centralized user management is needed.

When it comes to performance, NFS generally outperforms SMB in Linux and UNIX environments due to its simpler design and lower overhead. NFS has been optimized for the types of operations commonly performed on UNIX-like systems, such as reading and writing large files. This makes it a preferred choice for environments where large-scale data transfer and high-performance file access are necessary. SMB, in contrast, has historically been more complex and often incurs more overhead, particularly in Windows environments. However, the introduction of SMB2 and SMB3 has significantly improved its performance, especially in modern Windows systems where high-performance file sharing is required. SMB now supports larger buffers, pipelined requests, and multi-channel communication, making it more suitable for environments that require efficient access to files over a network, particularly in mixed OS environments.

The choice between NFS and SMB often comes down to the specific use case and the operating systems involved in the network. In environments dominated by UNIX or Linux systems, NFS is often the protocol of choice. Its simplicity, performance, and ability to seamlessly integrate with UNIX-like file systems make it an ideal solution for file sharing between Linux servers and clients. NFS is particularly useful for shared home directories, networked storage, and high-performance computing clusters, where large files need to be accessed and modified frequently. In these environments, the ability to mount remote directories and access them transparently across multiple systems is crucial.

SMB, on the other hand, is more commonly used in Windows-based environments. It is the default file sharing protocol in Windows and is integrated deeply into the Windows operating system. SMB is commonly used for file sharing in small office environments, enterprise networks, and homes where multiple Windows machines need to share files. It is also used for printer sharing and network communication in Windows environments. The advanced features of SMB, such as file locking and integration with Active Directory, make it an excellent choice for organizations using Microsoft services and infrastructure.

In mixed-OS environments, where both Windows and UNIX/Linux systems need to access shared files, SMB and NFS can be used together. Linux and UNIX systems can use Samba, an open-source implementation of SMB, to provide file sharing with Windows clients. Similarly, Windows systems can use NFS client software to access file systems shared by UNIX-based servers. This flexibility allows organizations to create hybrid environments where both NFS and SMB are used according to the needs of different systems.

Another important consideration when choosing between NFS and SMB is the ease of setup and management. NFS tends to be simpler to configure in UNIX/Linux environments, where it is natively supported and easily integrated into the system. Administrators can quickly set up NFS exports and mount points, and the protocol is highly customizable with various options for controlling access, performance, and security. SMB, while more feature-rich, can require more effort to set up and manage, especially in larger environments where Active Directory integration, user management, and security policies are involved. In mixed environments, managing both NFS and SMB can add complexity, but tools like Samba help streamline this process.

Ultimately, the decision to use NFS or SMB depends on the specific requirements of the network and the operating systems in use. NFS remains the protocol of choice for high-performance file sharing in UNIX and Linux environments, while SMB is the preferred option for

Windows-based systems and mixed environments. Both protocols have their strengths, and understanding their differences and use cases allows organizations to implement the right solution for their file sharing needs. Whether prioritizing performance, security, or compatibility, both NFS and SMB provide robust solutions for sharing files across networks.

Introduction to Cron Jobs

Cron jobs are an integral part of the UNIX-like operating systems, allowing users and administrators to schedule tasks to be executed automatically at specific times or intervals. This feature is particularly useful for automating repetitive tasks, such as system maintenance, backups, log rotations, or any other tasks that need to run periodically. Cron jobs are powered by the cron daemon, a background process that runs continuously, checking the cron table (crontab) for scheduled tasks and executing them when the time comes. Understanding how cron jobs work, how to configure them, and the various options available can significantly enhance system automation and management.

At its core, a cron job is a scheduled command or script that is executed at a defined time. The cron daemon uses the crontab file, which is a configuration file containing the schedule for the tasks to run. This file can be edited by any user on the system to specify when and what commands should be executed. Each line in the crontab file represents a single job and consists of six fields that define the timing and the command to be executed. The fields include the minute, hour, day of the month, month, day of the week, and the command to run. By specifying the appropriate values for these fields, users can schedule tasks to run at very specific times or intervals.

The crontab syntax is quite flexible, allowing for precise scheduling. For example, a cron job can be set to run every day at a certain time, every week on a specific day, or even every minute if needed. The timing fields follow a simple format where numbers or wildcards are used to represent different times and intervals. For instance, a cron job set to run at 2:30 PM every day would look like 30 14 * * *

/path/to/command. Here, the 30 represents the minute, the 14 represents the hour in a 24-hour format, and the asterisks represent any day of the month, any month, and any day of the week.

The crontab file can be edited by running the crontab -e command, which opens the user's crontab file in a text editor. Each user has their own crontab file, and these files are stored in the /var/spool/cron/crontabs directory on most systems. The crontab file is also specific to the user who owns it, meaning that a user can only edit their own crontab, not the crontab of other users unless they have superuser (root) privileges. In addition to the crontab file, system-wide cron jobs can be configured in /etc/crontab and various directories under /etc/cron.d/ for more centralized control of scheduled tasks.

One of the key features of cron jobs is their ability to run tasks automatically at scheduled intervals without requiring manual intervention. This can save time and effort for system administrators by automating routine tasks such as system backups, updates, and log management. For example, a cron job could be used to back up important files at 2 AM every day, ensuring that data is regularly backed up without the need for a user to initiate the process. Similarly, log rotation can be automated to occur at regular intervals, preventing log files from growing too large and consuming excessive disk space.

Cron jobs can also be set up for more complex tasks, such as running system monitoring scripts or executing custom scripts for application maintenance. For instance, a cron job could be scheduled to check the health of critical services every hour and send alerts if any service is down. This level of automation helps ensure that critical tasks are handled promptly and efficiently, without requiring constant human oversight.

While the power of cron jobs is in their ability to automate repetitive tasks, there are many additional features and options available that can further enhance their functionality. For instance, cron allows users to specify environment variables that can be used within their jobs. These variables can define paths, user credentials, or other settings that might be required for the execution of a command. Additionally, the standard output (stdout) and standard error (stderr) of cron jobs can be redirected to log files, allowing for easy monitoring of job execution and troubleshooting in case of failures. By default, cron sends the output of a job to the user's email address, but this behavior can be configured to redirect output to a file or suppress it entirely.

The use of cron jobs is not limited to system administrators. Regular users can also take advantage of cron to automate personal tasks. For example, a user might schedule a cron job to remind them of important tasks or to automatically download files from the internet at a specific time each day. By providing a simple and flexible way to automate tasks, cron can improve productivity and streamline workflows for users across different levels of an organization.

However, there are some considerations to keep in mind when working with cron jobs. One of the common challenges is managing time zones. Cron jobs are typically executed based on the system's local time, so if the system is set to a different time zone than the user expects, it may cause jobs to run at unintended times. In multi-user environments or when working across different time zones, it is important to ensure that all cron jobs are scheduled with the correct time zone in mind to avoid confusion.

Another consideration is ensuring that the environment in which cron jobs run is correctly configured. Unlike commands executed interactively by users, cron jobs do not load the user's environment settings automatically. As a result, environment variables such as $PATH, $USER, or custom variables may not be available to the cron job unless they are explicitly defined in the crontab file. If the cron job relies on specific environment settings, these must be specified within the cron job definition to avoid errors.

Despite these challenges, cron remains an incredibly powerful tool for automating system tasks and ensuring that routine operations are performed consistently and on time. Its flexibility in scheduling and executing tasks has made it a staple of system administration across UNIX-like operating systems. By leveraging the features of cron jobs, administrators can reduce the manual effort required to maintain systems and ensure that critical tasks are handled automatically. Whether it's for system maintenance, data backups, or personal task automation, cron jobs provide a simple yet powerful solution for automating nearly any recurring task in a computer system.

Scheduling Tasks with Cron

Cron is an indispensable tool in UNIX-like operating systems, allowing users and system administrators to automate tasks that need to be run at specific intervals. By scheduling tasks with cron, repetitive tasks such as backups, system maintenance, or automated scripts can be executed at precise times without manual intervention. This automation ensures that critical tasks are carried out regularly and consistently, freeing up time for administrators and users to focus on more complex tasks. The core of cron's functionality is its ability to schedule commands or scripts to run at predefined times, which is done by editing a configuration file known as the crontab.

To schedule tasks with cron, the user must understand the syntax of the crontab file, where the timing of each task is defined. The crontab file consists of six fields: minute, hour, day of the month, month, day of the week, and the command or script to execute. These fields are separated by spaces or tabs, and the values in each field determine when the task will be triggered. The minute field specifies the exact minute of the hour when the task will run, ranging from 0 to 59. The hour field specifies the hour, with values ranging from 0 (midnight) to 23 (11 PM). The day of the month field specifies the day of the month, and the month field specifies which month of the year the task should run, with values from 1 (January) to 12 (December). The day of the week field determines which day of the week the task will run, with values ranging from 0 (Sunday) to 6 (Saturday). Finally, the command field is where the script or command to be executed is placed.

Understanding how to use these fields allows for precise control over when tasks are scheduled. For example, if a task needs to run every day at midnight, the crontab entry would look like this: 0 0 * * * /path/to/script. In this case, the 0 0 represents midnight (0 minutes and 0 hours), the asterisks indicate that the task should run every day of the month, every month, and on any day of the week. If the task is intended to run once a week, say every Monday at 3 AM, the crontab entry would be 0 3 * * 1 /path/to/script. Here, the 1 in the day of the week field represents Monday, so the task would execute at 3 AM on every Monday.

Cron allows for a great deal of flexibility in task scheduling. For instance, a task could be set to run every five minutes by using */5 in the minute field, resulting in the entry */5 * * * * /path/to/script. Similarly, tasks can be scheduled to run on specific days of the week. For example, to run a task every Tuesday and Thursday at 4 PM, the crontab entry would be 0 16 * * 2,4 /path/to/script, where 2,4 in the day of the week field specifies Tuesday and Thursday. The flexibility provided by cron allows administrators to fine-tune the scheduling of tasks to meet the specific needs of their environment.

When working with cron, users should be aware of some advanced features that can enhance task scheduling. One such feature is the use of multiple commands in a single cron job. This can be achieved by using a semicolon to separate commands within the command field. For example, a user may want to run two commands consecutively: 0 1 * * * command1; command2. This will run command1 at 1 AM, followed by command2 after command1 finishes. This ability to chain commands can be useful for tasks that involve multiple steps, such as cleaning up old files and backing up data.

Another advanced feature is the use of the @reboot directive in crontab. This allows tasks to be run automatically each time the system reboots. For example, @reboot /path/to/script will execute the specified script each time the machine starts up. This feature is especially useful for starting background services or performing system checks immediately after a reboot.

In addition to scheduling tasks in the crontab file, users can set environment variables for cron jobs. By default, cron jobs run in a limited environment with a minimal set of environment variables. If the scheduled task relies on specific environment variables, such as a custom PATH or other variables, these must be explicitly set in the crontab file. For example, if a cron job needs to run a script that relies on a custom PATH, the user can specify this in the crontab by setting the PATH variable like this: PATH=/usr/local/bin:/usr/bin:/bin. This ensures that the cron job will be able to locate all necessary executables.

Cron jobs can also generate output, which by default is sent to the user's local email address. However, this can be redirected to a file or suppressed entirely if desired. For example, adding >/dev/null 2>&1 to the end of a cron job entry will discard both standard output and standard error, while redirecting the output to a log file can help with troubleshooting and monitoring. For instance, the entry 0 3 * * * /path/to/script >> /var/log/my_script.log 2>&1 will append the output of the script to a log file located at /var/log/my_script.log, capturing both normal output and error messages.

Despite its power and flexibility, there are a few common pitfalls that users should be mindful of when scheduling tasks with cron. One of the most frequent issues arises from incorrect time zone handling. By default, cron uses the system's local time zone, which can cause confusion if the system is set to a different time zone than expected. For users working in multiple time zones, it is important to account for time zone differences when setting cron schedules. Additionally, cron jobs often run with a minimal environment and may not have the same user environment variables that are available when running commands interactively. This can lead to problems when scripts or commands rely on certain variables, such as PATH or USER, which are not set automatically. In these cases, it is necessary to explicitly define the required environment variables in the crontab.

Cron is a powerful tool for automating tasks, and it can help users streamline system administration by scheduling regular jobs that would otherwise require manual intervention. By understanding the syntax and capabilities of cron, users can effectively manage recurring tasks such as backups, system updates, and file maintenance, ensuring that these processes run on schedule and without error. Whether it is running a system check every day, cleaning up temporary files every week, or executing custom scripts at specific intervals, cron is an indispensable tool for task automation in UNIX-like systems.

Cron Syntax and Time Formats

Cron is a powerful tool in UNIX-like operating systems, enabling users and administrators to automate tasks by scheduling them to run at specific times or intervals. Understanding cron syntax and time formats is essential for effectively using this tool. The crontab file, which defines when tasks should be executed, follows a particular syntax that consists of several time and command fields. The crontab file uses a simple but flexible format that allows users to schedule tasks as precisely as needed, from running a task every minute to executing it only on specific days of the week. The time format within the crontab is central to its operation, and knowing how to configure it can ensure that tasks run exactly when required.

At its core, a cron job consists of six fields. The first five fields are used to define the schedule, while the sixth field specifies the command or script to be executed. These fields include minute, hour, day of the month, month, and day of the week. Each of these fields can be filled with specific values or wildcards, which allows for a great deal of flexibility in scheduling. The values in these fields are used by the cron daemon to determine when the associated task should run.

The minute field specifies the exact minute during the hour when the cron job will run. It can take values from 0 to 59. If a cron job is set to run at minute 0, it will execute at the beginning of every hour. For example, a cron job set to run at minute 5 of every hour would have a minute value of 5. The hour field is similarly defined, with values ranging from 0 to 23, where 0 represents midnight, 1 represents 1 AM, and so on until 23, which represents 11 PM. For instance, to schedule a cron job to run at 2:30 AM every day, the entry would read 30 2 * * *. This means the job will run at the 30th minute of the second hour each day.

The day of the month field is used to define the specific day of the month when the cron job will execute. The values in this field range from 1 to 31, and a wildcard (*) can be used to indicate that the job should run every day of the month. For example, * * 15 * * would schedule a cron job to run on the 15th day of every month, no matter what day of the week it falls on. The month field specifies which month the cron job should run. This field ranges from 1 to 12, where 1 represents January and 12 represents December. If a cron job is set to run every month, a wildcard (*) can be used in this field, so the job will execute every month of the year.

The day of the week field is used to specify which days of the week the job should run. This field takes values from 0 to 6, where 0 corresponds to Sunday, 1 to Monday, and so on until 6, which corresponds to Saturday. A common use of this field is to schedule tasks for specific weekdays. For example, if you want a cron job to run every Monday at 3 AM, the entry would be 0 3 * * 1. By combining values from the day of the month and the day of the week fields, users can fine-tune the execution times of their cron jobs. For example, a cron job that runs on the first Monday of every month at 6 PM would be written as 0 18 1-7 * 1, indicating that it should run at 18:00 (6 PM) between the 1st and 7th day of the month, but only if the day is a Monday.

The flexibility of cron scheduling is enhanced by the ability to use special characters in the fields. One of the most commonly used special characters is the asterisk (*), which represents any value. When placed in a field, it tells cron to execute the job for every possible value of that field. For example, a cron job with * * * * * would run every minute of every hour, every day of the month, every month, and every day of the week. This is useful for tasks that need to run continuously, such as monitoring processes or checking system health. Another special character is the comma (,), which allows users to specify multiple values in a field. For instance, 0 12 * * 1,5 would run the job at noon on both Monday and Friday. The hyphen (-) is used to define a range of values, such as 1-5, which would specify days of the week from Monday to Friday. This can be useful for tasks that should run on a specific range of days, like scheduling a task to run from the 1st to the 15th of every month.

The slash (/) is another important character in cron syntax. It is used to define intervals. For example, */5 * * * * would run a job every 5 minutes, as the slash is combined with the value 5 to indicate an interval of 5. This character allows tasks to be scheduled at fixed intervals, such as every hour or every day, depending on the field it is placed in. Additionally, it can be used in combination with ranges to execute tasks at regular intervals within a specific range of values. For instance, 0 9-17/2 * * * would run a job every two hours between 9 AM and 5 PM, specifically at 9 AM, 11 AM, 1 PM, 3 PM, and 5 PM.

Cron's versatility extends beyond simple scheduling. It can also handle the execution of complex tasks and scripts. For example, you can schedule multiple commands to be run sequentially by using semicolons between them. Similarly, redirecting the output of cron jobs to a file is a common practice, allowing users to capture logs or debug information. Cron will automatically email the output of the job to the user who created the cron job, unless redirected to a file or suppressed.

Cron jobs provide a robust way to automate repetitive tasks in a UNIX-based system. Understanding the cron syntax and time formats is essential for effectively using this tool to schedule tasks. By manipulating the various fields and special characters, users can fine-tune the timing of their jobs to match their specific needs. From simple hourly tasks to complex weekly schedules, cron provides the flexibility and power needed to automate virtually any repetitive task, making it an indispensable tool for system administrators and users alike. By learning the syntax and mastering the use of special characters, users can schedule tasks with precision and efficiency, streamlining their workflows and improving the overall management of their systems.

Cron Directories and Configuration Files

Cron is an essential tool for automating scheduled tasks in UNIX-like operating systems. It helps system administrators and users to execute tasks automatically at defined intervals, saving time and effort. While many users interact with cron through the crontab command and the crontab file, there are several directories and configuration files involved in the cron system that are crucial to its operation. Understanding these directories and configuration files can provide deeper insight into how cron functions and how it can be customized and managed.

The crontab file is the most widely known configuration file associated with cron. Each user, including the root user, has their own crontab file, which contains the schedule and commands for that user's cron jobs. These files are typically stored in the /var/spool/cron/crontabs directory on most systems. This directory holds the individual crontab files for each user, and the crontab entries in these files specify when certain tasks should be run and what commands should be executed. Users can interact with their personal crontab files using the crontab command, which allows them to edit, list, and remove cron jobs.

The crontab file follows a very specific syntax that must be adhered to in order for the cron daemon to process the scheduled tasks correctly. Each line in the crontab represents a single cron job, which consists of six fields. The first five fields define the schedule for the job—minute, hour, day of the month, month, and day of the week—while the last field contains the command or script to be executed. The crontab file itself can be edited by running the crontab -e command, which opens the user's crontab file in the default text editor. Once edited, the file is saved, and the cron daemon automatically picks up the changes without requiring a restart. Cron jobs defined in a user's crontab file run with the permissions of that user, which is important for security and access control.

In addition to user-specific crontab files, there is a system-wide crontab file located in the /etc/crontab directory. This file is typically used to define cron jobs that are intended to run for the system as a whole, such as periodic system maintenance tasks. The system-wide crontab is structured similarly to user-specific crontab files, but it includes an additional field that specifies the user under which the command should run. This field is necessary because system cron jobs are often executed by different users depending on the task. For example, a system job like log rotation might be scheduled to run as the root user, while a task such as clearing temporary files might run as a non-privileged user.

The /etc/crontab file is more powerful in some respects because it allows system-wide tasks to be scheduled for the entire system, rather than just for individual users. This makes it ideal for system maintenance tasks that need to be executed regularly, such as updates, backups, or cleanup operations. Because the system-wide crontab affects the entire system, it is essential that only trusted administrators have access to this file to prevent unauthorized changes that could compromise system security.

Another important directory related to cron is the /etc/cron.d/ directory. This directory is used for placing cron job files that follow a similar format to the system-wide crontab, but the files in /etc/cron.d/ are typically used for specific tasks or packages. For example, if a software package is installed on the system and it requires scheduled tasks to be run periodically, it might create a file in the /etc/cron.d/

directory to define those tasks. The crontab file format in /etc/cron.d/ is identical to the system-wide crontab, but the advantage of using this directory is that it allows for better organization of cron jobs. By keeping package-specific cron jobs in separate files within /etc/cron.d/, administrators can easily manage and maintain these tasks without cluttering the primary crontab files.

Inside the /etc/cron.d/ directory, each file represents a separate cron job definition, and each file can define multiple cron jobs. For example, a cron job that runs a cleanup script every hour might be stored in a file named cleanup, and the file would contain the cron job definition for that task. The filenames in this directory are arbitrary, but they should be descriptive and indicate the task the file is responsible for. This organization makes it easy for administrators to see which cron jobs are related to specific applications or system services.

The /etc/cron.d/ directory is also where some automated systems place their scheduled tasks when they are installed, and administrators can manually add cron job definitions to this directory as needed. As with the system-wide crontab file, it is crucial that the files in /etc/cron.d/ are carefully managed to avoid unintended changes or security risks. Files in /etc/cron.d/ must be carefully structured and must follow the correct syntax to ensure that they are processed by the cron daemon correctly.

Cron also utilizes several directories for managing specific types of cron jobs. For instance, there are directories such as /etc/cron.daily/, /etc/cron.weekly/, /etc/cron.monthly/, and /etc/cron.hourly/ that provide a more convenient way to schedule tasks that run on specific time intervals. These directories allow administrators to place scripts that should run once a day, week, month, or hour, and cron automatically picks up these scripts and executes them according to the defined schedule. These directories offer a simple, organized way to manage common tasks such as log rotation, system cleanup, or report generation without having to manually edit crontab files.

In addition to the configuration files and directories mentioned above, there are a number of cron-related configuration files that control the behavior of the cron daemon itself. These files include /etc/crontab, /etc/cron.deny, and /etc/cron.allow. The cron.allow and cron.deny files are used to manage which users are permitted to run cron jobs. The cron.allow file specifies a list of users who are allowed to create and run cron jobs, while the cron.deny file lists users who are explicitly denied access to cron functionality. These access control files can help prevent unauthorized users from creating or modifying cron jobs, which is particularly important in multi-user environments.

Cron's versatility makes it a powerful tool for system administrators, but managing cron jobs effectively requires knowledge of its various configuration files and directories. By organizing cron jobs into user-specific crontabs, the system-wide crontab, and the /etc/cron.d/ directory, administrators can ensure that tasks are executed according to the desired schedule and that the system runs smoothly without unnecessary manual intervention. Proper management of cron directories and configuration files is critical for keeping the system organized, secure, and efficient, enabling automation to work seamlessly across the entire environment.

Managing Cron Job Permissions and Access

Cron jobs are powerful tools for automating tasks in UNIX-like systems, enabling administrators to schedule repetitive or system-wide tasks to run at specified times. While cron jobs are useful for automating processes such as backups, updates, and routine system maintenance, it is crucial to manage the permissions and access associated with these jobs to maintain security and prevent unauthorized actions. Proper management of cron job permissions ensures that only authorized users can schedule or execute certain tasks, and it also prevents accidental or malicious modifications that could compromise system integrity.

Cron job permissions and access control are managed in several ways, primarily through the configuration of user-specific crontab files, system-wide crontab files, and the use of specialized access control files like /etc/cron.allow and /etc/cron.deny. Each of these components plays a role in regulating who can create, modify, or execute cron jobs, and understanding how they work together is essential for maintaining secure cron job management.

The crontab command allows individual users to define their own cron jobs by editing their user-specific crontab file. Each user on the system has their own crontab file, which is stored in the /var/spool/cron/crontabs directory. The contents of a user's crontab file determine the commands and scripts that will run at the specified times. The default behavior of cron allows each user to manage their own cron jobs, meaning they can schedule tasks, edit their crontab files, or remove scheduled tasks without affecting other users.

However, this flexibility can be problematic if users have access to modify or create cron jobs that could interfere with system operations or access sensitive data. For this reason, it is important to implement control over who can create and modify crontab files. The system administrator can manage access by using the /etc/cron.allow and /etc/cron.deny files, which explicitly define which users are permitted to run cron jobs and which users are denied access. These files provide a mechanism for controlling access to cron functionality based on the system's user accounts.

The /etc/cron.allow file is used to specify a list of users who are explicitly allowed to create and modify cron jobs. If this file exists, only users listed in it will be able to schedule cron jobs. This helps ensure that only authorized users have the ability to schedule tasks that could affect system performance or security. If a user is not listed in the /etc/cron.allow file, they will be prevented from creating or editing cron jobs, regardless of their user privileges. This level of control is especially useful in multi-user systems where different individuals may have varying levels of access to the system.

On the other hand, the /etc/cron.deny file lists users who are explicitly denied access to cron jobs. If a user's name appears in this file, they will not be able to create or manage cron jobs, even if they are part of the system's user group. The /etc/cron.deny file can be used to block specific users from accessing cron, providing an additional layer of control. However, it is important to note that if both /etc/cron.allow and /etc/cron.deny files exist on the system, the cron daemon will prioritize the /etc/cron.allow file. In other words, if a user is in the cron.allow file, they will be granted access, even if they are listed in the cron.deny file.

The permissions associated with user-specific crontab files are another important aspect of cron job access control. Each user's crontab file must have the correct file permissions to ensure that only the user and authorized system administrators can modify or view the file. Crontab files are typically owned by the user they belong to, and only the root user or the specific user should be able to modify or access their respective crontab file. This prevents unauthorized users from modifying the crontab file of other users, which could potentially lead to unauthorized tasks being executed.

The default file permissions for crontab files ensure that only the root user or the owner of the file has write access, while others have read-only access or no access at all. The crontab command itself ensures that users can only modify their own crontab file, preventing them from editing files belonging to other users. If an administrator needs to modify the cron jobs of another user, they can do so by using the crontab -e -u username command, which allows the root user to edit the crontab file of any other user. This command can be useful for system administrators when making system-wide changes to scheduled tasks, but it should be used with caution to prevent unauthorized modifications.

In addition to user and system-wide crontab files, cron also supports the use of the /etc/crontab file and the /etc/cron.d/ directory, which are used for system-level tasks. These files allow the system administrator to schedule cron jobs that affect the entire system, such as log rotation, backup tasks, or scheduled updates. Unlike user-specific crontab files, the /etc/crontab file contains an additional field that specifies the user under which each task should run. This feature is useful for scheduling tasks that need to be run with specific user privileges. However, since these files control system-wide tasks, they should be carefully managed to ensure that unauthorized users do not gain access to sensitive system tasks.

By managing permissions and access to cron jobs, system administrators can prevent unauthorized access and ensure that tasks are executed securely. The use of /etc/cron.allow and /etc/cron.deny files, along with proper file permissions for crontab files, helps to maintain a secure environment where cron jobs are only accessible to authorized users. In multi-user environments, it is particularly important to ensure that users cannot create or modify cron jobs that could interfere with the functioning of the system or compromise its security.

Additionally, administrators must be aware of the potential risks associated with running cron jobs as the root user. While running tasks as the root user provides greater privileges, it also increases the risk of executing malicious or erroneous commands that could damage the system. For this reason, it is advisable to limit the use of root-level cron jobs and ensure that only trusted and necessary tasks are scheduled with root privileges. By following best practices for cron job permissions and access control, administrators can leverage the full power of cron while keeping their systems secure and well-managed.

Debugging Cron Jobs: Logs and Errors

Cron jobs are an essential tool for automating system tasks, yet even the most carefully scheduled jobs can encounter errors. These errors may arise from incorrect syntax, environment variables, permission issues, or other unforeseen system-related problems. When a cron job fails or does not behave as expected, it can be frustrating for administrators who rely on cron to perform routine tasks such as backups, system maintenance, or data processing. Fortunately, debugging cron jobs is a systematic process that involves examining the logs, analyzing error messages, and reviewing the configuration files. By using the available debugging tools, administrators can identify the root causes of cron job failures and take the necessary steps to resolve them.

When debugging cron jobs, one of the first places to look is the system's log files. Cron jobs typically generate output, including error messages or logs that can help administrators identify what went wrong. These logs are usually found in system log files such as /var/log/syslog or /var/log/messages on most UNIX-like operating systems. These logs contain entries that record when cron jobs are started, when they finish, and any errors or warnings that occur during execution. For example, if a cron job fails to run due to incorrect syntax or permission issues, the logs may provide clues as to why the task did not execute as intended. By examining the logs in detail, administrators can trace the sequence of events leading up to the failure and identify any relevant error messages that may point to the problem.

In addition to system logs, cron jobs also generate their own output, which can be captured and redirected to specific log files for easier debugging. By default, cron sends the output of its jobs to the user's email address, but this can be redirected to a file or suppressed entirely. To ensure that cron jobs generate useful logs, administrators can modify the cron job definition to include output redirection. For instance, appending >> /path/to/logfile 2>&1 to a cron job's command ensures that both the standard output (stdout) and standard error (stderr) are written to the specified log file. This allows administrators to track the job's execution and catch any errors that occur during runtime. Redirection is especially useful for long-running or complex cron jobs that need to generate logs for monitoring or troubleshooting purposes.

Another critical aspect of debugging cron jobs is understanding the environment in which they run. Cron jobs are executed in a minimal environment, which means that they do not have the same environment variables as a user's interactive shell. As a result, cron jobs may encounter errors if they rely on specific environment variables, such as $PATH, $USER, or custom variables, that are not available by default. For example, a cron job that calls a script may fail if the script requires a command that is not in the cron job's minimal $PATH. To resolve such issues, administrators can explicitly define the necessary environment variables within the cron job's configuration. For example, including PATH=/usr/local/bin:/usr/bin:/bin at the beginning of the cron job can ensure that the script can access the required binaries. This helps avoid errors caused by missing or misconfigured environment variables.

In addition to environment variables, permission issues are another common cause of cron job failures. Cron jobs run with the privileges of the user who created them, and this can result in access or permission-related problems if the job tries to execute actions or access files that the user does not have permission for. For example, a cron job may fail if it attempts to write to a directory that the user does not have write permissions for, or if it tries to access a network resource that requires elevated privileges. One way to troubleshoot permission issues is to check the ownership and permissions of the files and directories involved in the cron job. It may also be helpful to review the specific commands or scripts that the cron job is running to ensure that the user has the appropriate permissions to execute those tasks.

Another potential source of errors in cron jobs is the configuration of the cron schedule itself. The crontab file follows a strict syntax that defines when each job will run. A common issue arises from incorrect timing or formatting in the crontab entry. For example, a cron job may be scheduled to run every hour at minute 0 (0 * * * *), but if the minute field is incorrectly set, the job may not run as expected. It is important to ensure that the cron syntax is correctly followed and that all fields are appropriately defined. For instance, an incorrect range or an improperly placed comma can prevent the cron job from executing. To debug scheduling issues, administrators can examine the crontab entry carefully and ensure that the syntax aligns with the desired schedule.

In some cases, cron jobs may fail to run if the cron daemon itself is not functioning correctly. The cron daemon, which is responsible for executing cron jobs, must be running for scheduled tasks to be executed. If the cron daemon is not running or has encountered an error, it will not be able to process the cron jobs. To check the status of the cron daemon, administrators can use the systemctl command on systems that use systemd, or the service command on older systems. If the cron daemon is not running, restarting the service may resolve the issue. Additionally, if the cron daemon encounters any internal errors, these may be logged in system log files such as /var/log/syslog, which can help identify the source of the problem.

If a cron job involves complex scripts or commands, debugging may require more detailed inspection of the script's behavior. Administrators can test the script manually by running it directly from the command line, which can help identify syntax errors, missing dependencies, or issues with specific commands. If the script runs successfully from the command line but fails when executed as a cron job, this may indicate an issue with the cron environment, such as missing environment variables or file permissions. In such cases, it may be useful to add debugging statements to the script, such as echo commands or logging, to trace its execution and capture any errors that occur during the cron job's run.

Finally, cron job failures can sometimes be caused by system resource limitations. If the system is running low on memory, CPU, or disk space, cron jobs may be unable to execute or may fail unexpectedly. Monitoring system resources during cron job execution can help identify whether resource constraints are impacting the successful execution of tasks. Using tools like top, htop, or vmstat can provide real-time information about system resources, and administrators can take corrective actions if necessary, such as freeing up disk space or optimizing system performance.

Debugging cron jobs is an essential skill for maintaining a stable and efficient system. By checking logs, reviewing cron job configurations, ensuring proper permissions, and testing scripts, administrators can troubleshoot and resolve errors effectively. This proactive approach to managing cron jobs ensures that automated tasks run smoothly and that system administration remains efficient and error-free.

Advanced Cron Scheduling: Using reboot, daily, and More

Cron is a powerful tool for automating tasks on UNIX-like systems, but its true potential is unlocked when users take advantage of its advanced scheduling capabilities. While cron's basic syntax allows for specifying specific times or intervals for executing tasks, more advanced features offer greater flexibility and convenience. These advanced features, including the ability to schedule jobs based on system reboot, daily executions, and other time-based triggers, allow system administrators to fine-tune task automation and make the most of the cron daemon's capabilities. Understanding how to use these advanced scheduling options enhances the utility of cron and ensures that tasks are executed at the optimal time.

One of the most useful advanced cron scheduling features is the ability to execute jobs upon system reboot. This is particularly helpful for tasks that need to run only when the system starts up, such as initializing services, cleaning temporary files, or performing health checks. Cron offers a special keyword for this purpose, @reboot, which schedules a job to run each time the system reboots. When a job is scheduled with the @reboot keyword, it does not require a specific time or interval, as it is triggered by the system's reboot process. For example, adding an entry like @reboot /path/to/script to the crontab will execute the specified script every time the machine starts.

Using @reboot can be advantageous for administrators who need to ensure that certain tasks or services are set up immediately after the system boots. This is especially useful in environments where specific applications or processes need to be automatically started without user intervention. Furthermore, @reboot is often used in conjunction with other cron scheduling options, such as setting environment variables or running startup scripts, to ensure that the system is ready for use as soon as it finishes rebooting.

In addition to the @reboot option, cron also offers keywords such as @daily, @hourly, @weekly, and others, which provide convenient shorthand for commonly scheduled tasks. These keywords simplify the process of scheduling tasks to run at regular intervals, reducing the need to manually specify the minute, hour, day, and so on. For example, @daily is a shorthand for scheduling a job to run once every day at midnight. It is equivalent to specifying o o * * * in the crontab file. Using @daily makes the crontab entry more readable and eliminates the need to remember the specific time values for midnight, making it easier to configure tasks such as daily backups, system checks, or log rotations.

The @hourly keyword is another commonly used option. It schedules a task to run once every hour, and it is equivalent to the cron entry o * * * *. This is particularly useful for tasks that need to run frequently but not necessarily on a precise minute within each hour. For example, a system administrator might use @hourly to schedule a script that monitors system performance or checks disk usage every hour. By using the @hourly keyword, the administrator can quickly set up regular checks without having to manually define the specific timing values.

Similarly, the @weekly keyword schedules jobs to run once a week, typically on Sundays at midnight. This is useful for tasks that need to be executed on a weekly basis, such as running backups, clearing temporary files, or updating system databases. The use of @weekly simplifies scheduling weekly maintenance tasks, ensuring that they are performed consistently without requiring manual input each week.

In addition to the built-in keywords, cron also allows users to define more complex scheduling patterns using the standard cron syntax. This flexibility enables tasks to be executed at a wider range of intervals, such as specific days of the month, certain months of the year, or particular days of the week. For example, a user may want to run a task on the first Monday of every month. Instead of manually calculating the date and specifying it in the cron expression, the user can simply write 0 3 * * 1 to schedule the task for 3 AM on every first Monday. This flexibility makes cron a powerful tool for managing recurring tasks in a precise and controlled manner.

Cron's advanced scheduling features also extend to the ability to set custom intervals within specific time ranges. The slash (/) operator can be used to define an interval between specific values. For instance, a user might want to schedule a task to run every 15 minutes. Rather than manually specifying every minute value (e.g., 0,15,30,45), they can use the */15 syntax in the minute field, resulting in a cron job that runs every 15 minutes. This feature is particularly useful for tasks that need to be repeated at regular intervals within a specific time range, such as monitoring or logging tasks.

The ability to specify ranges of values also adds to cron's versatility. By using the hyphen (-) operator, users can define a range of values for specific fields. For example, scheduling a job to run between 9 AM and 5 PM every weekday could be achieved with the entry 0 9-17 * * 1-5. This ensures that the task runs during business hours on weekdays without needing to list each individual hour. Similarly, using a comma (,) allows users to specify multiple, discrete values. For example, scheduling a job to run at 3 AM on Mondays, Wednesdays, and Fridays can be accomplished with 0 3 * * 1,3,5.

Advanced cron scheduling is not only about setting precise times; it also enables more efficient resource management. By automating routine tasks at specific intervals or upon system reboot, administrators can ensure that important processes are executed consistently and without human intervention. This reduces the likelihood of errors or oversights, such as missing backups or failing to clean up temporary files, that could affect system performance or data integrity.

Cron's advanced features also integrate seamlessly with system management tools. For example, many Linux distributions use cron jobs for log rotation. By scheduling log rotation tasks using the @daily keyword or other cron syntax, administrators ensure that logs do not consume excessive disk space over time. Similarly, automated backups can be scheduled at off-peak hours, such as early in the morning, to minimize the impact on system performance during business hours.

Moreover, cron jobs are not limited to system maintenance tasks. They can be used for a wide variety of applications, including automating user-specific tasks, running scripts for data processing, or executing machine learning models at set intervals. The versatility of cron's scheduling options makes it an invaluable tool for managing everything from simple administrative tasks to complex workflows in highly dynamic environments.

By taking advantage of cron's advanced scheduling features such as @reboot, @daily, @hourly, and custom time intervals, system administrators can efficiently manage automated tasks and ensure the smooth operation of systems. The simplicity of the cron syntax combined with its powerful scheduling capabilities allows administrators to create complex, recurring automation schedules with minimal effort, making it a critical tool for routine system management and performance optimization.

Cron vs Systemd Timers: Differences and Use Cases

In UNIX-like operating systems, automating repetitive tasks is crucial for ensuring smooth system operations. Two powerful tools that enable task automation are cron and systemd timers. Both serve similar purposes in that they allow tasks or scripts to be scheduled and executed at specific times or intervals. However, while cron has been the traditional tool for task scheduling for many years, systemd timers offer a modern alternative with some distinct advantages and additional features. Understanding the differences between cron and systemd timers, as well as their respective use cases, is essential for system administrators when deciding which tool best fits their automation needs.

Cron is a widely used job scheduler that has been a part of UNIX-like operating systems for decades. Its simple, text-based configuration and flexible time-based syntax make it a popular choice for automating system tasks, from routine maintenance to periodic backups. Cron jobs are typically defined in a user's crontab file, which contains a series of time-based expressions and corresponding commands or scripts to execute. Each line in the crontab file represents a single cron job, with fields specifying when the job should run (minute, hour, day of the month, month, and day of the week). This straightforward syntax and the familiarity of cron make it an easy tool to configure and use, particularly for simple recurring tasks.

Systemd, on the other hand, is a system and service manager used by modern Linux distributions. It has become the default initialization system for many Linux systems, replacing older systems such as SysVinit. Systemd includes a variety of features designed to improve system management, including service management, process supervision, logging, and resource control. One of the features added with systemd is systemd timers, which provide functionality similar to cron but with additional capabilities integrated into the systemd ecosystem. Systemd timers allow administrators to schedule tasks in a manner similar to cron but offer more flexibility in terms of dependency management, systemd unit integration, and status monitoring.

While both cron and systemd timers allow for the scheduling of tasks, their configuration, management, and capabilities differ in significant ways. One of the most noticeable differences is the underlying architecture. Cron is a standalone service that operates independently of the system's init system. It runs in the background as a daemon and processes jobs based on the user's crontab files. In contrast, systemd timers are a part of the systemd suite and are tightly integrated with the system's service management. This integration allows systemd timers to work seamlessly with other systemd features, such as service dependencies, logging, and resource management.

The configuration of cron jobs is relatively simple, with users editing their crontab files to specify when and what tasks should be executed. The crontab syntax is based on a set of time fields that define the schedule for the task, and cron will run the command or script specified in the crontab whenever the conditions are met. Cron's simplicity is both its strength and limitation. It is easy to use and configure for basic tasks, but it lacks the advanced features and integrations that systemd timers offer. Cron jobs run in a minimal environment, meaning that they do not have access to the same environment variables or system resources as the user's interactive session. This can lead to issues when cron jobs rely on specific environment settings, such as a custom $PATH or other user-specific variables.

Systemd timers are configured using systemd unit files, which are more powerful and flexible than cron's simple text configuration. A systemd timer consists of two unit files: a timer unit and a service unit. The timer unit defines when the task should be triggered, while the service unit specifies the command or script to be executed. This separation of the timer and service allows for greater flexibility, such as scheduling tasks with complex dependencies or chaining multiple tasks together. Systemd timers also allow administrators to specify conditions under which a task should run, such as requiring that a service be active or that certain resources be available.

One key advantage of systemd timers is their ability to manage dependencies between tasks. For example, a systemd timer can be configured to run only after a specific service has started or only if a certain system resource is available. This is particularly useful in scenarios where one task depends on the successful completion of another, ensuring that tasks are executed in the correct order. In contrast, cron lacks this capability, as each cron job runs independently of others, with no built-in way to manage dependencies or check the status of services.

Another important feature of systemd timers is the ability to track the status and execution of scheduled tasks. Systemd provides detailed logs for all tasks, including cron-like jobs scheduled with timers. These logs are integrated into the systemd journal, allowing administrators to easily track the success or failure of a task and troubleshoot any issues. Cron, on the other hand, does not provide built-in logging capabilities. While cron jobs can be configured to send output to a file or email, this setup is more manual and less integrated into the system's overall logging infrastructure. This makes systemd timers a more robust choice for tasks that require detailed logging or need to be monitored closely for errors.

Systemd timers also support more advanced scheduling options compared to cron. While cron uses a simple syntax based on time fields, systemd timers allow for more granular control over when tasks are triggered. For example, systemd timers support the ability to run tasks with specific intervals, such as once every 10 minutes or every 2 hours. Systemd timers also support a concept known as "drift" tolerance, which allows tasks to be triggered with some flexibility in timing, accommodating situations where the system may not be running exactly on time or when tasks need to be triggered after a certain delay.

Despite the advantages of systemd timers, cron remains a useful tool, especially for simple, independent tasks that do not require the advanced features offered by systemd. Cron's simplicity makes it well-suited for environments where the tasks to be automated are straightforward and do not involve complex dependencies or integration with other services. It is also widely supported across many different UNIX-like systems, including older distributions that may not use systemd.

Systemd timers, however, are increasingly becoming the preferred choice in modern Linux environments, particularly on systems that use systemd as the init system. The integration of timers with systemd's service management, logging, and resource control features makes them a more powerful and flexible option for administrators who need to manage complex automation tasks. The ability to manage dependencies, track task execution, and integrate with the system's service management tools makes systemd timers particularly suited for enterprise environments or systems where task automation requires more control and visibility.

The decision to use cron or systemd timers ultimately depends on the specific requirements of the tasks being automated and the underlying system architecture. Cron remains an excellent choice for simpler, independent tasks, while systemd timers offer a more robust, feature-rich solution for complex automation needs that require system integration and detailed logging. Both tools are invaluable for automating repetitive tasks, and understanding their differences allows system administrators to choose the right tool for the job.

Cron Alternatives: Anacron and at Command

While cron is a powerful and widely used tool for scheduling tasks on UNIX-like operating systems, it may not always be the best fit for every situation. Cron relies on the system's clock to trigger jobs at specified times, meaning that tasks that are missed due to the system being powered off or idle when a job is supposed to run may not be executed at all. This limitation can be problematic in certain use cases, especially for systems that do not run 24/7 or need to ensure that tasks run even after being offline for extended periods. In such cases, alternative tools like Anacron and the at command offer useful solutions for managing scheduled tasks that are not suitable for cron's traditional time-based approach.

Anacron is a utility specifically designed to complement cron by addressing the issue of missed jobs due to system downtime. Unlike cron, which operates strictly based on system time and requires the system to be running at the scheduled time, Anacron allows jobs to be executed even if the system was not running when they were supposed to. This is particularly useful for tasks on laptops, desktops, or other systems that may not be powered on continuously or may be shut down for extended periods. Anacron ensures that tasks scheduled to run at regular intervals, such as daily, weekly, or monthly jobs, are executed as soon as the system is next running.

Anacron works by specifying how frequently a task should run, rather than scheduling it for a specific time of day. For example, an Anacron job might be scheduled to run every day, but instead of defining an exact time, the system will run the task the next time it boots up if it was missed. This makes Anacron ideal for systems that are not always on at the same time each day or week. Anacron jobs are configured by editing the /etc/anacrontab file, where administrators define the frequency of the task and the command to execute. In this file, tasks are assigned a frequency, such as "1" for daily, "7" for weekly, and "30" for monthly. Anacron will then execute the job when the system starts, ensuring that the task is completed, even if the scheduled time was missed.

Anacron differs from cron in that it does not rely on precise scheduling with timestamps. Instead, it tracks the number of days since the last execution and ensures that a task runs at least once within the specified frequency, but without requiring the system to be running at a specific time. For example, if a job is scheduled to run every day, but the system is off for three days, Anacron will execute the job the moment the system starts up again, making up for the missed runs. Anacron is particularly useful for tasks such as daily backups, disk cleanup, or routine system maintenance that need to run regularly, but are not dependent on running at specific times.

While Anacron is great for tasks that need to run with a flexible schedule, the at command provides another alternative that is more suited to one-time tasks or tasks that need to run once at a specific time in the future. The at command allows users to schedule a task to run at a specific time, once, and it offers a simple and straightforward method for one-off jobs that do not require repetition. Unlike cron and Anacron, which are designed to handle recurring tasks, the at command is useful when a task needs to run at a particular time, such as sending an email, triggering a system process, or running a script after a delay.

The at command is ideal for scenarios where an immediate or delayed task needs to be scheduled and executed once. For instance, if an administrator needs to run a maintenance script at midnight or trigger a data backup after a set period, the at command can be used to schedule these one-off events. The syntax for using the at command is simple, with the user specifying the command to execute and the time when the command should run. For example, entering at 2:00 PM will allow the user to input a command that will be executed precisely at 2:00 PM on the same day. Additionally, users can specify times in relative terms, such as at now + 1 hour, which would schedule a task to run one hour from the current time.

At jobs are stored in the /var/spool/at directory, and users can view a list of scheduled at jobs by running the atq command. If necessary, administrators can remove a scheduled job with the atrm command, followed by the job number from the output of atq. Unlike cron jobs, which are automatically executed by the cron daemon at predefined times, at jobs are executed by the atd daemon, which checks for scheduled jobs and runs them at their specified time. This makes the at command ideal for tasks that need to be executed only once at a specific time, such as running a script after a system update or scheduling a task during off-peak hours to minimize impact on system resources.

Both Anacron and the at command offer solutions to scheduling tasks in situations where cron's typical functionality may fall short. Anacron is excellent for ensuring that jobs run regularly, even if the system is offline during their scheduled execution time. This makes it ideal for systems that are not always on or that need tasks to be executed when the machine comes back online, such as routine backups or system maintenance. On the other hand, the at command is perfect for one-time tasks or tasks that must run at a specific time in the future, allowing for more flexibility in scheduling and execution.

However, it is important to note that while both Anacron and at provide alternatives to cron, they are not necessarily replacements for it. Cron remains the best tool for tasks that need to run at fixed intervals or on an exact schedule. Anacron and at are meant to supplement cron in cases where it may not be the best fit. For example, cron would still be the tool of choice for recurring tasks that need to run at specific times, while Anacron is better suited for tasks that need to be completed within a certain timeframe but can afford to be delayed, and at is better for one-time or future scheduling needs.

Ultimately, Anacron and the at command provide system administrators with the flexibility to manage task scheduling in environments where cron alone may not be sufficient. By understanding the strengths and limitations of these tools, administrators can choose the right solution for their specific use cases, ensuring that system maintenance, backups, and other automated tasks are executed with precision and reliability. These alternatives, combined with cron, allow administrators to manage tasks across a variety of scenarios, making task automation more adaptable and efficient.

Automating System Maintenance with Cron

Automating system maintenance tasks is an essential part of managing a healthy and efficient computer system. One of the most effective tools for automating these tasks on UNIX-like systems is cron. Cron allows administrators to schedule tasks to run at specific times or intervals, eliminating the need for manual intervention. With the power of cron, tasks such as system backups, log rotation, updates, and cleanup can be performed consistently and reliably, ensuring that a system remains operational and secure. By automating these routine processes, system administrators can focus on more complex tasks while minimizing the risk of errors or oversight.

System maintenance involves a variety of tasks, ranging from cleaning up temporary files to updating software packages and ensuring that logs do not grow too large. Many of these tasks need to be executed on a regular basis, such as daily, weekly, or monthly. Cron is ideally suited to handle this type of automation, as it allows administrators to schedule commands and scripts to run at predetermined times. The cron daemon runs in the background and checks the crontab file for scheduled jobs, executing them when the specified time arrives. The crontab file contains a series of entries that define the timing and the command to run, allowing for precise control over task execution.

One of the most common system maintenance tasks that can be automated with cron is log rotation. As applications and system services generate logs, those logs can grow quickly and consume large amounts of disk space. If logs are not properly managed, they can fill up the available storage, causing system performance issues or even system crashes. To prevent this, administrators often configure log rotation, a process that archives old logs and creates new log files. Log rotation can be set up to occur on a daily, weekly, or monthly basis, depending on the volume of logs generated. By automating log rotation with cron, administrators can ensure that logs are regularly rotated, preventing storage issues and keeping the system running smoothly.

Another important system maintenance task that cron can automate is system updates. Keeping a system up-to-date is critical for maintaining security, performance, and stability. Many operating systems and package managers allow administrators to schedule automatic updates, ensuring that the system remains patched with the latest security fixes and software improvements. Cron can be used to run scripts that check for updates and install them at regular intervals, such as every night or every week. For example, a cron job can be scheduled to run a package manager like apt, yum, or dnf, checking for and installing updates automatically. This automation ensures that the system is always protected against known vulnerabilities without requiring manual updates.

In addition to log rotation and system updates, cron can be used for other essential system maintenance tasks such as cleaning up temporary files, checking disk usage, and monitoring system health. Temporary files, such as cache files or application-specific files, can accumulate over time and take up valuable disk space. Cron jobs can be scheduled to periodically clean these files, ensuring that the system does not run out of space. For example, a cron job can be set to delete temporary files in the /tmp directory or clear out cache files from web browsers or application directories. Similarly, disk usage can be monitored and managed by setting up cron jobs that alert administrators when disk space reaches a certain threshold. By automating disk checks and cleanup, administrators can prevent issues caused by insufficient storage space.

Cron can also be used to automate tasks related to system performance and monitoring. For example, cron jobs can be scheduled to run scripts that monitor the health of system resources such as CPU usage, memory, and disk I/O. These scripts can log performance data or send alerts when thresholds are exceeded, allowing administrators to address potential issues before they impact system stability. Monitoring system performance and resource utilization is a critical part of system maintenance, and automating this with cron ensures that the system is regularly checked without manual intervention.

Another critical system maintenance task that can be automated with cron is database backups. For systems running databases such as MySQL, PostgreSQL, or SQLite, regular backups are essential for data protection. Cron can be used to schedule backup jobs that create database snapshots or export data to a backup file. These backups can then be stored locally or remotely to ensure that data is safe in case of system failure. Scheduling regular backups with cron is a simple way to protect data without requiring constant manual oversight. Depending on the importance of the data, backups can be scheduled to run daily, weekly, or even hourly, ensuring that the most recent data is always available in case of failure.

Cron's flexibility extends beyond simple system maintenance tasks. It can also be used to automate complex workflows that involve multiple steps. For example, a system administrator might want to run a series of maintenance tasks such as cleaning up logs, checking disk space, and sending an email report to the user or administrator. By using cron to schedule these tasks, administrators can automate entire workflows, ensuring that each step occurs in the correct order and at the right time. These workflows can be written as shell scripts or other executable programs that are then scheduled to run at specified times with cron.

To configure cron jobs for system maintenance, administrators typically edit the crontab file. The crontab file contains the schedules for the jobs and is edited by running the crontab -e command. The file consists of several fields: minute, hour, day of the month, month, day of the week, and the command to execute. These fields allow administrators to define the exact timing for each task. For example, a cron job that runs a log rotation script every Sunday at 3 AM might have the following entry in the crontab file: 0 3 * * 0 /path/to/logrotate-script. This entry would trigger the script to run at 3:00 AM every Sunday.

Cron's ability to schedule tasks with such precision allows for efficient and reliable system maintenance. It ensures that routine tasks are performed on time, without requiring constant manual intervention. This level of automation reduces the risk of human error, ensures that critical tasks such as backups and updates are consistently performed, and helps administrators maintain the overall health of the system.

By leveraging cron to automate system maintenance, administrators can ensure that their systems remain secure, optimized, and well-maintained with minimal effort. The automation of routine tasks allows administrators to focus on higher-level system management, troubleshooting, and other complex tasks while trusting that the system will handle its regular maintenance efficiently. Cron's role in system maintenance continues to be indispensable, providing administrators with the tools to keep systems running smoothly and effectively.

Understanding Sysctl and Kernel Parameters

Sysctl is a powerful tool in UNIX-like operating systems, including Linux, for configuring and managing kernel parameters at runtime. The kernel is the core component of the operating system, responsible for managing hardware, system resources, and communication between software and hardware. Kernel parameters control various aspects of the system's behavior, such as networking, memory management, process scheduling, and security. Sysctl provides a user-friendly interface to access and modify these parameters, allowing system administrators to fine-tune the operating system's performance and functionality without requiring a system reboot.

The sysctl utility allows administrators to view and modify kernel parameters dynamically, meaning that changes can take effect immediately without needing to restart the system. This makes sysctl a critical tool for managing system performance, tuning network settings, and adjusting kernel settings in real-time. Kernel parameters are organized into a hierarchical structure, where each parameter corresponds to a specific aspect of the kernel's behavior. Sysctl can be used to modify these parameters by reading from and writing to files within the /proc/sys/ directory, which provides a virtual interface to the kernel.

The syntax for interacting with sysctl is simple. To view a kernel parameter's current value, the sysctl command is used followed by the parameter name. For example, running sysctl net.ipv4.ip_forward would display the current value of the ip_forward parameter, which controls whether the system can forward network packets. To modify a parameter, the sysctl command can be used with the -w option, followed by the parameter name and the desired value. For example, sysctl -w net.ipv4.ip_forward=1 would enable IP forwarding on the system. This dynamic configuration is particularly useful in environments where changes need to be applied without downtime, such as in high-availability systems or production environments.

Sysctl parameters are grouped by categories, such as networking, process control, and memory management. Networking parameters control how the system interacts with network interfaces and handles data transmission. For example, the net.ipv4.tcp_max_syn_backlog parameter determines the maximum number of pending connections that the TCP stack will allow during the connection setup phase. Modifying this parameter can help optimize networking performance, especially in systems that handle a large number of incoming connections, such as web servers or database servers. Similarly, the net.ipv4.ip_forward parameter controls whether the system can route packets between different networks, which is essential for systems acting as routers or gateways.

Memory management is another critical area where sysctl plays a vital role. Kernel parameters related to memory management control how the system handles memory allocation, swapping, and caching. For instance, the vm.swappiness parameter controls the tendency of the system to use swap space instead of physical RAM. A low value for swappiness tells the kernel to prefer using RAM over swap, which can improve performance on systems with sufficient memory. Conversely, a higher swappiness value can be set on systems with limited physical memory to encourage the kernel to swap data out to disk more aggressively, preventing out-of-memory conditions.

Sysctl also provides control over process scheduling, which determines how the system allocates CPU time to running processes. The kernel.sched_min_granularity_ns parameter, for example, defines the minimum amount of time a process must run before the scheduler can preempt it to give CPU time to another process. This setting is important for managing system responsiveness, particularly on multi-core processors or systems running real-time applications. By adjusting the scheduling parameters through sysctl, administrators can balance system responsiveness and throughput to meet the needs of specific workloads.

In addition to real-time performance adjustments, sysctl is also crucial for enhancing system security. Many kernel parameters are designed to limit access to sensitive resources or prevent certain types of attacks. For example, the fs.suid_dumpable parameter controls whether core dumps are generated for set-user-ID (SUID) programs, which can expose sensitive data from privileged processes. By disabling core dumps for SUID programs, system administrators can reduce the risk of sensitive information being exposed in the event of a crash. Similarly, the kernel.dmesg_restrict parameter controls access to the kernel's ring buffer, which contains log messages generated by the kernel. Restricting access to these logs can prevent unauthorized users from obtaining potentially sensitive information about the system's internal workings.

Sysctl configurations are often set temporarily through the sysctl command, but these changes are not persistent across reboots by default. To make changes permanent, administrators can modify the /etc/sysctl.conf file, which contains a list of sysctl parameters and their values. Any changes made to this file will be applied automatically during the system startup, ensuring that the desired kernel settings are applied consistently after a reboot. In addition to the sysctl.conf file, administrators can also place configuration files in the /etc/sysctl.d/ directory, where individual files can be used to override or set specific parameters. This directory-based approach offers more flexibility, particularly in systems that require different configurations based on specific use cases or environments.

Sysctl's flexibility and power make it an indispensable tool for managing system performance and behavior. It allows administrators to fine-tune kernel settings to optimize network throughput, memory usage, process scheduling, and security. However, modifying kernel parameters with sysctl requires caution, as improper settings can lead to instability, performance degradation, or security vulnerabilities. It is essential to test changes in a controlled environment before applying them to production systems, especially when modifying parameters related to memory management, networking, or process scheduling.

Sysctl is also a valuable tool for troubleshooting system performance issues. By monitoring kernel parameters in real-time, administrators can identify potential bottlenecks or misconfigurations that may be affecting system performance. For example, if a system is experiencing high latency or network congestion, administrators can use sysctl to check parameters related to network buffers or TCP settings. Adjusting these parameters can help alleviate the issue without the need for a system reboot. Similarly, monitoring memory usage with sysctl can help administrators identify excessive swapping or memory fragmentation, allowing for proactive tuning to prevent out-of-memory conditions.

In complex environments, sysctl can be integrated with other system monitoring and management tools to automate the process of adjusting kernel parameters based on real-time metrics. For instance, if a system's memory usage exceeds a certain threshold, a monitoring tool could trigger a script that modifies the vm.swappiness parameter to optimize memory usage. This integration allows for dynamic system adjustments based on workload patterns, improving overall system efficiency and responsiveness.

Sysctl and kernel parameters offer an advanced level of control over system behavior and performance. By understanding the intricacies of sysctl and its associated kernel parameters, system administrators can fine-tune their systems to meet specific requirements, whether optimizing for performance, security, or resource management. With the ability to modify kernel parameters dynamically, sysctl becomes a powerful tool for maintaining the health and stability of a UNIX-like operating system.

Basic Sysctl Configuration and Tuning

Sysctl is a command-line utility in UNIX-like operating systems that allows administrators to view and modify kernel parameters at runtime. These parameters are central to managing various aspects of system performance, including networking, memory management, process scheduling, and security. By configuring sysctl settings, administrators can optimize the behavior of the kernel to meet specific system requirements or enhance the overall performance and security of a machine. Understanding the basic sysctl configuration and tuning process is essential for system administrators who wish to fine-tune their systems to perform efficiently and reliably.

Sysctl works by reading and writing to virtual files within the /proc/sys/ directory, which contains the kernel parameters exposed by the system. These parameters control different aspects of the system, such as networking stack behavior, memory management, file system settings, and process handling. Sysctl allows administrators to view the current values of these parameters, and more importantly, to change them dynamically without requiring a system reboot. This provides great flexibility, especially in production environments where uptime is critical, and changes need to take effect immediately.

A key aspect of sysctl tuning is the ability to modify kernel parameters to optimize the system for specific workloads. For example, in high-performance networking environments, adjusting certain networking parameters can improve throughput, reduce latency, and prevent packet loss. The sysctl command is used to adjust these parameters. To view the current value of a kernel parameter, the basic syntax is sysctl parameter_name. For instance, to check the current setting for IP forwarding, you would run sysctl net.ipv4.ip_forward, which would return either a 0 or 1, indicating whether IP forwarding is enabled or disabled.

To change a kernel parameter with sysctl, administrators use the sysctl -w option followed by the parameter and the desired value. For example, if you want to enable IP forwarding, the command sysctl -w net.ipv4.ip_forward=1 would set the ip_forward parameter to 1, allowing the system to forward network packets. The changes made using sysctl -w take effect immediately, but they are not persistent across reboots unless saved to the configuration files.

Sysctl also allows the modification of settings related to memory management, which is essential for optimizing system performance. One of the parameters that can be tuned is vm.swappiness, which controls how aggressively the system swaps memory pages to disk. The value of this parameter ranges from 0 to 100, with lower values indicating a preference for using physical memory and higher values indicating a greater willingness to swap to disk. For example, on systems with a large amount of physical memory, setting vm.swappiness=10 could help avoid unnecessary swapping, which can improve performance by keeping more data in memory.

Another important memory-related parameter is vm.dirty_ratio, which controls the percentage of system memory that can be filled with dirty pages before the kernel starts writing them to disk. By adjusting vm.dirty_ratio, administrators can influence the system's disk I/O performance. A higher value may increase write performance by delaying writes to disk, but it can also lead to greater memory usage and longer I/O operations. By tuning these parameters, administrators can achieve a better balance between memory utilization and disk performance, particularly in environments with heavy read/write activity.

Sysctl also provides the ability to adjust process scheduling parameters, which is crucial for managing system responsiveness and efficiency. For example, the kernel.sched_min_granularity_ns parameter controls the minimum amount of time that a process must run before the kernel can preempt it to give CPU time to another process. This setting can be adjusted to control how responsive the system is to new processes. Lower values allow for more frequent context switches, making the system more responsive but at the cost of increased overhead. Conversely, higher values reduce context switches, which can improve throughput but may lead to less responsiveness in certain environments.

Networking parameters are another key area where sysctl configuration and tuning are essential. For example, the net.ipv4.tcp_max_syn_backlog parameter controls the maximum number of pending connections that can be queued during the TCP connection setup phase. Increasing this value can help prevent connection drops in high-traffic environments, such as web servers or database servers. Another important networking parameter is net.core.somaxconn, which determines the maximum number of connections that can be handled by the system's listening sockets. By increasing this value, the system can handle more incoming connections without rejecting them, which is crucial for systems that experience heavy traffic.

Sysctl also offers security-related parameters that allow administrators to harden the system against attacks. For example, the fs.suid_dumpable parameter controls whether core dumps are generated for set-user-ID (SUID) programs. By setting this parameter to 0, administrators can prevent core dumps from being created for SUID programs, thereby reducing the risk of exposing sensitive information from privileged processes. Similarly, the kernel.dmesg_restrict parameter controls access to the kernel's ring buffer, which contains log messages generated by the kernel. Restricting access to this buffer can prevent unauthorized users from accessing sensitive system information.

Sysctl parameters can be modified temporarily during runtime using the sysctl -w command, but these changes are not persistent across reboots unless saved to the system configuration files. To make sysctl changes permanent, administrators must edit the /etc/sysctl.conf file or place configuration files in the /etc/sysctl.d/ directory. The /etc/sysctl.conf file contains a list of kernel parameters and their values, and any changes made to this file will be applied automatically at system startup. By adding custom kernel parameter settings to this file, administrators ensure that the desired configurations are applied every time the system boots.

For systems that require specific kernel parameters for different use cases, the /etc/sysctl.d/ directory can be used to place configuration files that override or set specific parameters. This directory provides greater flexibility, as it allows administrators to manage different kernel parameter configurations based on system requirements or specific environments. For example, different sysctl settings might be needed for production systems, test environments, or development machines. By using the /etc/sysctl.d/ directory, administrators can easily manage and customize sysctl settings for different scenarios.

To apply sysctl settings manually, administrators can run the sysctl -p command, which reloads the /etc/sysctl.conf file and applies any changes that have been made. If configuration files are placed in the /etc/sysctl.d/ directory, the sysctl -p command will apply those as well. This process ensures that kernel parameter settings are consistently applied across system reboots.

Sysctl configuration and tuning are vital for optimizing system performance, security, and resource management. By understanding the various kernel parameters and how they impact system behavior, administrators can fine-tune their systems to meet the specific needs of their environments. Whether adjusting memory settings to improve performance, configuring networking parameters to optimize traffic handling, or implementing security measures to safeguard sensitive data, sysctl provides the tools necessary to manage and control the underlying behavior of the operating system.

Sysctl for Network Configuration

Sysctl is an essential tool for configuring and managing kernel parameters in UNIX-like operating systems, including Linux. It allows system administrators to modify kernel parameters at runtime, which can have a significant impact on system performance, security, and resource management. One of the most important areas where sysctl is used is network configuration. By adjusting sysctl parameters related to networking, administrators can optimize network performance, enhance security, and fine-tune the behavior of the networking stack. Understanding how to use sysctl for network configuration is crucial for managing high-performance, secure, and reliable networking in modern systems.

Networking in UNIX-like systems relies heavily on kernel parameters that govern how the system handles communication over the network. These parameters control everything from IP routing and packet forwarding to buffer sizes and connection timeouts. Sysctl provides a powerful interface to modify these settings without requiring a system reboot, making it ideal for real-time adjustments to network performance and behavior. Networking parameters in sysctl are typically grouped under the net namespace, which includes various subcategories for different aspects of networking, such as IPv4, IPv6, and TCP/IP settings.

One of the first and most important networking parameters that can be configured with sysctl is the net.ipv4.ip_forward parameter. This parameter controls whether the system can act as a router, forwarding IP packets between different networks. By default, most systems do not forward packets, meaning they are limited to sending and receiving traffic only within their local network. However, in cases where the system needs to route packets between different subnets or to provide gateway functionality, the ip_forward parameter must be set to 1. This is particularly useful for systems configured as firewalls, routers, or network gateways, where packet forwarding is essential. The command sysctl -w net.ipv4.ip_forward=1 would enable IP forwarding, while sysctl -w net.ipv4.ip_forward=0 would disable it.

Sysctl also allows administrators to configure network security settings that help protect the system from malicious network traffic. For example, the net.ipv4.tcp_syncookies parameter enables TCP synchronization cookies, which help protect against SYN flood attacks, a common type of Denial-of-Service (DoS) attack. When set to 1, this parameter activates SYN cookies, which prevent attackers from exhausting the system's resources by flooding it with a large number of half-open TCP connections. This feature can be crucial in securing high-traffic systems from certain types of network attacks. Administrators can enable this feature by running sysctl -w net.ipv4.tcp_syncookies=1.

Another important aspect of network configuration is the size of the kernel's network buffers, which determine how much data can be buffered in memory during network transmission. By adjusting these buffer sizes, administrators can improve network throughput, particularly in environments that handle large volumes of traffic. For instance, the net.core.rmem_max and net.core.wmem_max parameters control the maximum receive and send buffer sizes, respectively. These parameters can be adjusted to allow for larger buffers, improving performance on systems that handle high-bandwidth operations, such as file servers or databases. To increase the maximum buffer size for receive operations, an administrator might run sysctl -w net.core.rmem_max=16777216 to set the maximum receive buffer size to 16 MB.

Additionally, sysctl provides several parameters related to TCP connections, which are crucial for managing network traffic and improving the efficiency of network communication. The net.ipv4.tcp_max_syn_backlog parameter, for example, controls the maximum number of pending connections that the kernel will allow during the TCP connection establishment phase. Increasing this value can be helpful for servers that experience a high volume of incoming connection requests, as it reduces the likelihood of connections being dropped due to the backlog queue being full. To increase the maximum number of pending connections, the command sysctl -w net.ipv4.tcp_max_syn_backlog=4096 can be used, which sets the backlog size to 4096.

The net.ipv4.tcp_fin_timeout parameter controls how long the system waits before it can reuse a TCP connection in the TIME_WAIT state. In high-performance network environments, reducing the timeout value can improve the system's ability to quickly reuse connections, which is especially beneficial for web servers or other services that handle many short-lived connections. Administrators can adjust this value by running sysctl -w net.ipv4.tcp_fin_timeout=30, which sets the timeout to 30 seconds. This reduces the time the system waits before closing connections, thus freeing up resources more quickly for new incoming connections.

In addition to performance-related parameters, sysctl is also used to manage networking settings for IPv6. The net.ipv6.conf.all.disable_ipv6 parameter, for example, controls whether IPv6 is enabled or disabled on the system. While IPv6 adoption has grown in recent years, there are still situations where IPv6 may need to be disabled for compatibility reasons or network configuration. To disable IPv6 on the system, the following command can be used: sysctl -w net.ipv6.conf.all.disable_ipv6=1.

Sysctl also allows for the fine-tuning of network interfaces on a per-interface basis. For example, parameters like net.ipv4.conf.etho.rp_filter control the reverse path filtering behavior on a specific network interface, such as etho. Reverse path filtering is a security feature that helps protect the system from IP spoofing by ensuring that incoming packets are received on the correct interface. Adjusting the rp_filter setting can help mitigate certain types of network-based attacks, particularly in complex network environments with multiple interfaces.

For systems that require high availability or need to handle network traffic during periods of peak load, sysctl provides several parameters for managing TCP congestion control. The net.ipv4.tcp_congestion_control parameter specifies which congestion control algorithm should be used by TCP connections. Common algorithms include cubic, reno, and bbr. The cubic algorithm is the default in many Linux systems and is designed to optimize throughput in networks with high bandwidth and long delays. However, the newer bbr (Bottleneck Bandwidth and Round-trip propagation time) algorithm has been shown to improve performance in high-latency and high-loss environments. To change the congestion control algorithm, an administrator can run sysctl -w net.ipv4.tcp_congestion_control=bbr.

Sysctl also plays an important role in managing IPv4 and IPv6 route tables, such as configuring how the system handles network traffic routing. By adjusting parameters like net.ipv4.route.gc_interval, which controls the frequency of route garbage collection, administrators can optimize the system's routing table management, reducing unnecessary overhead or ensuring that routing information is kept up-to-date.

Sysctl offers a wide array of networking-related parameters that can be fine-tuned to meet the needs of specific system configurations. By adjusting these parameters, system administrators can optimize network performance, improve security, and ensure that their systems are well-suited for handling the demands of modern network traffic. Whether configuring basic network settings, improving security, or fine-tuning TCP and UDP traffic handling, sysctl provides the flexibility to tailor a system's network behavior to its specific requirements.

Managing Memory with Sysctl

Memory management is one of the most critical aspects of system performance in UNIX-like operating systems. Efficient memory management ensures that applications run smoothly, prevents memory exhaustion, and maintains system stability even under heavy workloads. Sysctl, a powerful utility for configuring kernel parameters at runtime, plays a significant role in managing memory on these systems. By using sysctl, administrators can fine-tune memory-related kernel parameters to optimize system performance, control swapping behavior, and manage memory resource allocation. Understanding how to leverage sysctl for memory management is essential for administrators aiming to maximize system efficiency and performance.

At the heart of sysctl memory management are several important kernel parameters that govern how the system handles memory allocation, paging, swapping, and caching. These parameters allow administrators to adjust system behavior in real time without requiring a reboot, providing flexibility in system tuning. One of the key memory-related parameters that sysctl can control is the vm.swappiness parameter. This setting defines how aggressively the kernel swaps out pages from physical memory to swap space on the disk when the system is under memory pressure. The swappiness value can range from 0 to 100, with lower values indicating a preference for using physical RAM, while higher values cause the kernel to swap to disk more readily.

The vm.swappiness parameter is particularly important for systems that have a large amount of RAM. On such systems, setting a low swappiness value, such as 10, tells the kernel to avoid swapping as long as possible, ensuring that most of the memory is used for active processes. This can improve performance, as accessing data from RAM is much faster than from disk. On the other hand, setting a higher swappiness value may be beneficial for systems with limited memory resources or environments where disk I/O is fast and swapping is less of a concern. Administrators can change this value dynamically by running the command sysctl -w vm.swappiness=10, which sets the swappiness value to 10.

Another key parameter for memory management is vm.overcommit_memory, which controls the kernel's behavior when allocating memory to processes. By default, Linux allows applications to request more memory than is physically available, potentially causing out-of-memory conditions or crashes. The vm.overcommit_memory parameter helps manage this behavior. It can be set to three possible values: 0 for the default heuristic (where the kernel guesses whether enough memory is available), 1 for always allowing overcommit (letting processes allocate memory even if there is not enough), and 2 for strictly checking memory allocation, ensuring that no process is granted more memory than what is available. Administrators can adjust this parameter by running sysctl -w vm.overcommit_memory=2 to enforce strict memory checks, preventing overcommitment and ensuring more predictable system behavior.

The vm.max_map_count parameter is another critical memory-related setting that controls the maximum number of memory map areas a process can have. This is important for applications that rely on memory-mapped files or use extensive memory for data processing. Increasing the value of vm.max_map_count can be beneficial for applications like databases or certain scientific computing applications that require large amounts of memory to be mapped into their address space. This parameter can be adjusted dynamically with sysctl -w vm.max_map_count=262144 to increase the number of allowed memory map areas.

Swapping behavior and memory overcommitment are crucial, but managing memory caches is equally important for system performance. Sysctl provides parameters that control how memory caches are handled to ensure that data is efficiently cached in memory without unnecessarily consuming too much space. The vm.vfs_cache_pressure parameter controls the kernel's aggressiveness when reclaiming memory from the virtual file system (VFS) cache. A high value for vfs_cache_pressure causes the system to reclaim VFS cache memory more aggressively, while a lower value tells the kernel to retain more VFS cache in memory. Tuning this value can be useful for systems that perform frequent file system access, where excessive memory consumption by the VFS cache might cause issues.

Similarly, the vm.drop_caches command provides administrators with the ability to clear caches manually. While it is not a typical use case for everyday management, clearing the page cache, dentries, or inodes can be useful in certain situations, such as when an administrator needs to free up memory after a significant file system operation. Running sysctl -w vm.drop_caches=3 clears the page cache, dentries, and inodes, freeing up memory resources. This is particularly useful on systems with constrained memory, where cache buildup might slow down performance or cause excessive swapping.

Sysctl also allows for the adjustment of kernel parameters related to direct memory access (DMA) and other low-level memory functions. For example, kernel.shmmax controls the maximum size of a shared memory segment. This is an important parameter for systems running applications that require large shared memory regions, such as databases or multi-threaded applications. By increasing the shmmax parameter, administrators can allocate more shared memory for processes, improving the performance of memory-intensive applications. The command sysctl -w kernel.shmmax=2147483648 would set the maximum shared memory segment size to 2 GB, allowing larger memory regions for applications that require them.

Managing memory in multi-core systems also involves controlling how memory is allocated to different CPU cores. Sysctl provides the vm.numactrls parameter, which determines how memory is assigned to specific CPU nodes in non-uniform memory access (NUMA) systems. In NUMA systems, memory is distributed across different nodes, and ensuring that processes access memory local to their CPU node can help optimize performance. By adjusting the vm.numactrls parameter, administrators can influence how memory is allocated in NUMA systems, ensuring that memory access is optimized for workloads that are sensitive to latency or bandwidth.

A related parameter is vm.zone_reclaim_mode, which controls whether the kernel attempts to reclaim memory from distant memory nodes on NUMA systems. Enabling zone reclaim can reduce latency by forcing the system to use memory local to the CPU, improving performance for memory-intensive tasks. This is an important feature for high-performance computing (HPC) environments where memory access time can significantly impact overall system performance.

As with other sysctl parameters, memory-related settings can be made persistent across system reboots. To make changes permanent, administrators can modify the /etc/sysctl.conf file or create custom configuration files in the /etc/sysctl.d/ directory. By adding memory tuning parameters to these files, administrators ensure that the settings are applied automatically every time the system boots, providing consistency and reliability for memory management.

Sysctl provides a wide range of memory-related parameters that allow administrators to fine-tune memory management for optimal system performance. Whether adjusting swap behavior, controlling memory overcommitment, or managing caches and NUMA settings, sysctl offers the flexibility and control needed to meet the demands of specific workloads and system configurations. By carefully managing memory with sysctl, administrators can improve system efficiency, prevent memory bottlenecks, and ensure that their systems remain stable and responsive under various conditions.

Changing Sysctl Parameters at Runtime

Sysctl is a powerful tool used in UNIX-like operating systems to control and manage kernel parameters at runtime. This tool allows administrators to modify kernel settings dynamically, which can be incredibly useful for tuning system performance, enhancing security, and adapting system behavior without the need to reboot. Changing sysctl parameters at runtime offers a significant advantage over traditional static configuration methods, especially when administrators need to fine-tune settings in response to changing workloads, system conditions, or performance requirements. Understanding how to modify sysctl parameters during system operation is essential for optimizing a system's performance and responsiveness.

When working with sysctl, the first step in changing kernel parameters at runtime is understanding the structure of these parameters and how they are organized. Kernel parameters are typically found in the /proc/sys/ directory, which provides a virtual filesystem that exposes various settings and parameters of the kernel. These parameters cover a broad range of system areas, including memory management, networking, process scheduling, and security. Sysctl interacts with this directory to view and modify parameter values, providing a simple and flexible interface to manage the kernel's behavior in real-time.

The sysctl command is used to read and modify these kernel parameters. To check the current value of a parameter, administrators use the sysctl command followed by the parameter name. For instance, running sysctl net.ipv4.ip_forward would return the current value of the ip_forward parameter, which controls whether the system is allowed to forward IP packets between different networks. The value of ip_forward can be either 0 (disabled) or 1 (enabled), depending on whether the system is configured as a router. This is an example of how sysctl provides immediate access to kernel settings, enabling quick inspection of system parameters.

To change a parameter, administrators can use the sysctl -w command, followed by the parameter name and the desired value. For example, to enable IP forwarding, an administrator would run sysctl -w net.ipv4.ip_forward=1. This command modifies the parameter's value in real-time, allowing the system to start forwarding packets immediately without requiring a reboot. Similarly, if an administrator wanted to disable IP forwarding, they would run sysctl -w net.ipv4.ip_forward=0. The ability to change kernel parameters at runtime without rebooting is particularly useful in production environments, where uptime is crucial, and changes need to be applied without interruption.

One of the main benefits of modifying sysctl parameters at runtime is the ability to quickly respond to system performance issues or changes in system behavior. For example, if a system is experiencing high latency due to networking congestion, an administrator might adjust parameters related to the TCP stack to optimize performance. The net.ipv4.tcp_rmem and net.ipv4.tcp_wmem parameters control the default and maximum sizes of the receive and send buffers for TCP connections, respectively. By increasing these buffer sizes, administrators can improve network throughput and reduce the impact of network congestion. These changes can be made instantly using sysctl commands, without needing to restart the system.

Memory management is another area where sysctl parameters are frequently modified at runtime. Parameters such as vm.swappiness and vm.overcommit_memory control the system's behavior when allocating and swapping memory. The vm.swappiness parameter, for example, determines how aggressively the kernel swaps memory pages to disk when physical RAM is under pressure. By adjusting this value, administrators can influence how the system handles memory usage during high-demand periods. A lower value for vm.swappiness tells the kernel to avoid swapping as much as possible, while a higher value makes the system more likely to use swap space. These adjustments can be made immediately with sysctl to optimize the system for specific workloads.

Additionally, sysctl allows for tuning of security-related parameters in real time. For example, the fs.suid_dumpable parameter controls whether core dumps are generated for set-user-ID (SUID) programs. In certain security-sensitive environments, administrators may want to disable core dumps for these programs to prevent sensitive information from being written to disk. The fs.suid_dumpable parameter can be modified instantly using the sysctl command, providing a quick way to enhance system security without rebooting. Similarly, other security-related settings, such as kernel.dmesg_restrict (which restricts access to kernel logs), can be changed at runtime to tighten system security when necessary.

For administrators who need to make persistent changes to kernel parameters, sysctl allows modifications to be written to configuration files, ensuring that settings are applied automatically at boot time. However, while changes made with the sysctl -w command are immediate, they are not persistent across reboots unless explicitly saved. To make changes permanent, administrators can modify the /etc/sysctl.conf file or create custom configuration files in the /etc/sysctl.d/ directory. These files contain key-value pairs that define the desired kernel settings, and when the system reboots, the values specified in these files are loaded into the kernel.

To ensure that sysctl settings are applied at boot time, administrators can run the sysctl -p command, which reloads the /etc/sysctl.conf file and applies any changes that have been made. For systems using the /etc/sysctl.d/ directory, the sysctl -p command will also apply changes from these configuration files. This mechanism ensures that sysctl settings are consistently applied across system reboots, making it easy to maintain a stable and optimized system configuration over time.

While modifying sysctl parameters at runtime is a powerful way to adjust system settings dynamically, it is important for administrators to approach these changes with caution. Incorrectly tuning sysctl parameters can have unintended consequences, such as degrading system performance, destabilizing the system, or introducing security vulnerabilities. It is crucial to thoroughly understand the impact of each kernel parameter before making changes, especially in production environments. Many sysctl parameters are interdependent, and modifying one setting may affect the behavior of others. Therefore, administrators should test changes in a controlled environment before applying them to critical systems.

Sysctl also provides a mechanism for administrators to monitor the status of kernel parameters in real time. By using the sysctl command without any arguments, administrators can view all kernel parameters and their current values. This is useful for monitoring system performance and verifying that parameters have been applied correctly. In addition, sysctl allows the use of tools like watch to continuously monitor specific parameters, providing real-time feedback on changes in system behavior.

The ability to modify kernel parameters at runtime using sysctl is one of the key features that makes UNIX-like systems so flexible and adaptable. Whether optimizing memory management, improving network performance, or enhancing system security, sysctl offers administrators a simple and effective way to tune system parameters without the need for downtime. By understanding how to change sysctl parameters at runtime and using these settings strategically, administrators can ensure that their systems perform optimally and meet the specific needs of their workloads.

Persistent Sysctl Configuration Across Reboots

Sysctl is a powerful tool used for configuring and managing kernel parameters in UNIX-like operating systems. These parameters control various aspects of system behavior, including memory management, networking, process scheduling, and security. While sysctl allows administrators to modify kernel settings dynamically, changes made at runtime are not persistent across reboots by default. As a result, administrators may need to apply these settings again after a system restart unless steps are taken to make the changes permanent. Understanding how to configure sysctl for persistence across reboots is crucial for ensuring that system performance, security, and configuration remain consistent after a restart.

The sysctl utility provides an easy-to-use interface to view and modify kernel parameters at runtime, but changes made using the sysctl -w command only last until the next reboot. For example, setting a parameter like vm.swappiness=10 using sysctl -w will immediately take effect, but it will be lost when the system is rebooted. To make changes persistent across reboots, administrators need to ensure that the kernel parameters are saved and re-applied automatically during the boot process.

The most common way to make sysctl changes persistent is by modifying the /etc/sysctl.conf file. This configuration file contains key-value pairs that represent sysctl parameters and their desired values. The file is read during the boot process, and the parameters defined within it are applied to the system automatically. To make sysctl changes permanent, administrators simply need to add the desired parameters and their values to this file.

For example, if an administrator wants to set the vm.swappiness parameter to 10 and make it persistent across reboots, they would add the following line to the /etc/sysctl.conf file:

vm.swappiness=10

This line will ensure that the swappiness parameter is set to 10 every time the system starts up. After making changes to the /etc/sysctl.conf file, administrators can apply the new settings immediately by running the sysctl -p command. This command reloads the /etc/sysctl.conf file and applies any changes that have been made, ensuring that the new parameters are applied without needing to reboot the system. The sysctl -p command is also useful for applying changes made to the file during runtime, allowing administrators to implement new settings on the fly.

In addition to /etc/sysctl.conf, the /etc/sysctl.d/ directory provides an alternative way to manage persistent sysctl settings. This directory allows administrators to create individual configuration files that contain sysctl settings, which can then be applied in a modular fashion. This approach is particularly useful when multiple sysctl configurations are required for different use cases or environments. Each file within /etc/sysctl.d/ can contain a set of kernel parameters that are applied when the system boots, making it easy to manage different configurations based on specific needs.

For example, a file named 99-custom.conf in the /etc/sysctl.d/ directory might contain custom kernel parameters for a specific application or environment. This file could contain settings like:

net.ipv4.ip_forward=1

vm.swappiness=10

When the system boots, all files in the /etc/sysctl.d/ directory are read, and the parameters within them are applied. This method allows for more granular control over sysctl settings, especially when managing complex configurations across different systems or environments.

To ensure that the changes made in the /etc/sysctl.d/ directory are applied, administrators can use the sysctl --system command. This command reads all configuration files, including /etc/sysctl.conf and any files in the /etc/sysctl.d/ directory, and applies the kernel parameters specified within them. The sysctl --system command is useful for ensuring that all sysctl settings are applied across the system and for applying changes made during runtime or during system startup.

While the /etc/sysctl.conf file and /etc/sysctl.d/ directory are the most common methods for ensuring persistent sysctl configuration, there are other mechanisms that can be used in specific scenarios. For example, some Linux distributions and system management tools may have their own configuration files or directories for managing sysctl settings. For instance, on systems using systemd, administrators may be able to define sysctl settings in systemd unit files, allowing for more advanced configuration and management.

Regardless of the method used, the key to making sysctl settings persistent is ensuring that the desired kernel parameters are saved to configuration files that are read and applied during the boot process. This guarantees that the system's configuration remains consistent across reboots and that any necessary parameters are applied automatically without requiring manual intervention after each restart.

It is important to note that while modifying sysctl parameters can optimize system performance and security, administrators should carefully consider the impact of each change before applying it to a production system. Some sysctl parameters, if misconfigured, can degrade system performance, create security vulnerabilities, or even cause system instability. Therefore, administrators should always test changes in a controlled environment before applying them to live systems. Additionally, it is advisable to document any changes made to sysctl settings, as this helps ensure that future system maintenance or troubleshooting efforts are based on a clear understanding of the system's configuration.

In some cases, administrators may need to revert sysctl settings to their default values after making changes. This can be done by commenting out the modified parameters in the configuration files or by using the sysctl -w command to reset individual parameters to their default values. The sysctl -w command allows for quick changes, but it is important to remember that these changes will not persist after a reboot unless they are saved to the appropriate configuration files.

The ability to make sysctl changes persistent across reboots is a critical part of system administration in UNIX-like environments. By configuring kernel parameters in a persistent manner, administrators can ensure that performance, security, and resource management settings are applied consistently across system reboots. Whether modifying memory management settings, optimizing networking parameters, or enhancing system security, sysctl provides a flexible and efficient way to manage kernel parameters and maintain a stable and optimized system. With the correct configuration, sysctl enables administrators to create systems that perform reliably and securely over time, even as workloads and requirements evolve.

Securing Systems with Sysctl Settings

Securing a system is one of the most critical tasks for system administrators, and kernel tuning plays a significant role in achieving this goal. Sysctl, a powerful command-line tool for configuring kernel parameters in real time, offers administrators a way to manage security-related kernel settings. By adjusting sysctl parameters, administrators can lock down systems, mitigate vulnerabilities, and protect against various types of attacks, all without needing to reboot the system. These security configurations help harden the kernel and restrict the potential attack surface, making sysctl an indispensable tool for securing UNIX-like operating systems.

The kernel, being the core of the operating system, is responsible for managing hardware resources, memory, processes, and system security. The kernel's default behavior may not always align with best security practices, particularly in a production environment or when the system is exposed to the internet. Fortunately, sysctl provides a set of parameters that can be tuned to enhance system security by restricting access to sensitive resources, controlling kernel logging, limiting the effects of network attacks, and more.

One of the first areas where sysctl can improve system security is by controlling access to kernel logs. The kernel logs, which can contain sensitive information about the system's operation, are often targeted by attackers trying to gather information about the system's configuration and potential vulnerabilities. By controlling access to the kernel's ring buffer, system administrators can prevent unauthorized users from viewing kernel logs. The kernel.dmesg_restrict parameter is used for this purpose. When set to 1, it restricts access to the kernel's dmesg log, making it only accessible to the root user. This can significantly reduce the risk of exposing sensitive information that might help an attacker exploit vulnerabilities. Setting sysctl -w kernel.dmesg_restrict=1 ensures that only privileged users can view these logs.

Another critical area where sysctl can enhance security is by controlling the behavior of the system with respect to core dumps. Core dumps are generated when a program crashes, and they contain a snapshot of the memory contents of the program at the time of the crash. While core dumps can be useful for debugging, they can also contain sensitive information, such as passwords, encryption keys, and other private data. In environments where security is a concern, it is essential to restrict the creation of core dumps for certain processes. The fs.suid_dumpable parameter controls whether core dumps are allowed for set-user-ID (SUID) programs, which are often targeted for exploitation by attackers. By setting fs.suid_dumpable to 0, administrators can disable core dumps for SUID programs, preventing the leakage of sensitive data. This can be done with the command sysctl -w fs.suid_dumpable=0.

Sysctl also provides the ability to control IP forwarding, a feature commonly used by attackers to perform network sniffing or to redirect traffic. The net.ipv4.ip_forward parameter controls whether the system forwards IP packets between network interfaces, which is essential for systems acting as routers or gateways. However, in a typical desktop or server environment, IP forwarding should be disabled to reduce the system's exposure to potential misuse. Setting sysctl -w net.ipv4.ip_forward=0 ensures that the system will not forward packets, reducing the risk of it being used in network-based attacks.

In addition to controlling IP forwarding, sysctl offers several parameters related to network security that help prevent Denial-of-Service (DoS) and Distributed Denial-of-Service (DDoS) attacks. One such parameter is net.ipv4.tcp_syncookies, which helps protect the system from SYN flood attacks. SYN flood attacks attempt to overwhelm a system by sending a large number of half-open TCP connections, consuming server resources and potentially causing system crashes. When net.ipv4.tcp_syncookies is set to 1, the kernel will use TCP SYN cookies to prevent this type of attack, ensuring that the system does not allocate resources until the connection is fully established. This setting can be enabled with sysctl -w net.ipv4.tcp_syncookies=1, providing an added layer of protection against network-based attacks.

Another important network-related parameter is net.ipv4.conf.all.rp_filter, which controls reverse path filtering. Reverse path filtering ensures that incoming packets come from the expected source and are received on the correct network interface. This helps mitigate IP spoofing, where an attacker sends packets with a forged source IP address. By setting net.ipv4.conf.all.rp_filter=1, administrators can enable strict reverse path filtering, preventing such spoofing attacks and ensuring that only valid packets are processed by the system.

Sysctl also allows administrators to limit the potential impact of buffer overflow attacks. The kernel.exec-shield and kernel.randomize_va_space parameters are designed to make it more difficult for attackers to predict the locations of critical system structures in memory, such as the stack or heap. These features make buffer overflow attacks harder to execute, as they randomize memory locations and implement additional protections against executing injected code. Setting sysctl -w kernel.randomize_va_space=2 enables full address space randomization, providing a robust defense against attacks that rely on predictable memory addresses.

In addition to addressing specific types of attacks, sysctl can also be used to implement more general hardening practices. For example, the kernel.randomize_va_space parameter, as mentioned earlier, randomizes the location of various memory segments to make it harder for attackers to exploit vulnerabilities related to predictable memory addresses. Similarly, the fs.protected_hardlinks and fs.protected_symlinks parameters can be used to prevent the creation of symbolic links or hard links that could be used maliciously to bypass security restrictions or access sensitive files.

Sysctl settings related to process control can also enhance system security. The kernel.pid_max parameter controls the maximum allowable process ID (PID) for the system. By reducing the maximum

PID value, administrators can limit the number of processes that can run concurrently, which may reduce the system's exposure to certain types of resource exhaustion attacks. Adjusting the kernel.pid_max value can be an effective strategy for securing systems that are not required to run large numbers of processes. The parameter can be adjusted dynamically with sysctl -w kernel.pid_max=65535.

For systems exposed to the internet or large networks, controlling the number of allowed open connections is another important security measure. The net.ipv4.tcp_max_syn_backlog parameter, which controls the maximum number of pending TCP connections, can be increased to help mitigate SYN flood attacks. Similarly, controlling the maximum number of open file descriptors with fs.file-max can limit the number of simultaneous open files and help prevent DoS attacks caused by resource exhaustion.

Securing a system requires more than just configuring a few sysctl parameters. It involves a combination of settings that govern various aspects of kernel behavior, including process control, memory management, network security, and file system protection. By using sysctl to fine-tune kernel parameters, administrators can implement a multi-layered defense strategy, reducing the attack surface and enhancing the overall security posture of the system. Whether through the use of access controls, randomization techniques, or specific network protections, sysctl provides the flexibility to harden systems against a wide range of potential threats.

Best Practices for Sysctl Optimization

Sysctl is an essential tool for configuring and managing kernel parameters in UNIX-like operating systems. The ability to modify kernel parameters dynamically provides system administrators with a powerful way to optimize performance, improve security, and fine-tune system behavior based on specific workloads and requirements. However, because sysctl parameters directly impact the kernel's operation, it is important to follow best practices when optimizing sysctl settings to avoid system instability, performance degradation, or unintended consequences. This chapter discusses some of the best practices for sysctl optimization, ensuring that administrators can configure their systems efficiently and securely.

One of the first steps in sysctl optimization is understanding the specific needs of the system. Not all sysctl parameters are relevant to every environment, and applying generic settings across the board can lead to suboptimal performance or unnecessary complexity. Before making any changes, administrators should evaluate the system's purpose, workload, and resource requirements. For example, a high-performance web server may require different networking settings compared to a database server or a system running scientific computations. By understanding the system's workload, administrators can focus on optimizing the parameters that will have the greatest impact on performance and efficiency.

A key aspect of sysctl optimization is ensuring that the right parameters are adjusted. There are numerous kernel parameters that control memory management, networking, process scheduling, and other critical aspects of the system's operation. When optimizing, administrators should focus on the parameters that most directly affect system performance for their specific use case. For instance, for systems with large amounts of memory, adjusting memory management parameters such as vm.swappiness and vm.overcommit_memory can help ensure that the system uses physical memory efficiently and avoids unnecessary swapping to disk. Similarly, adjusting networking parameters like net.ipv4.tcp_rmem and net.core.rmem_max can optimize throughput and reduce latency for high-traffic systems.

In addition to adjusting the relevant parameters, administrators should ensure that changes are made in a controlled and systematic way. Instead of making large-scale modifications to multiple sysctl settings all at once, it is advisable to implement changes incrementally and monitor their impact on system performance. After each change, administrators should use performance monitoring tools to assess the effect of the modification. Tools such as top, htop, vmstat, and netstat can provide real-time feedback on system resource usage and network activity, allowing administrators to determine if the optimization has achieved the desired effect. Incremental changes allow administrators to isolate the impact of each setting and make more informed decisions about further tuning.

When making sysctl changes, it is essential to balance performance optimization with system stability and security. Over-optimizing certain parameters can lead to adverse effects, such as resource exhaustion or increased vulnerability to attacks. For example, increasing buffer sizes (net.core.rmem_max) and reducing the swappiness value (vm.swappiness) may improve performance under high loads, but it could also lead to increased memory usage, causing the system to run out of memory in extreme cases. Likewise, enabling aggressive TCP parameters such as net.ipv4.tcp_fin_timeout could improve networking performance, but it may lead to issues with connections in certain use cases, especially on systems with a large number of simultaneous connections. Therefore, administrators should carefully test any optimization changes to ensure they strike the right balance between performance and stability.

Security is also a critical consideration when optimizing sysctl settings. Many kernel parameters influence system security, and adjustments that improve performance may inadvertently weaken the system's defenses. For example, disabling certain security features, such as the ability to generate core dumps for set-user-ID (SUID) programs by setting fs.suid_dumpable=0, can prevent an attacker from obtaining sensitive information in the event of a program crash. Similarly, enabling reverse path filtering with the net.ipv4.conf.all.rp_filter=1 setting helps mitigate IP spoofing and other network-based attacks. Sysctl can be used to harden the system by reducing the attack surface and ensuring that sensitive information is protected. Thus, it is essential to consider security implications when optimizing kernel parameters and ensure that performance improvements do not introduce vulnerabilities.

Another important best practice is to document sysctl changes clearly. Since kernel parameters directly affect system behavior, keeping a record of any modifications is crucial for troubleshooting, system auditing, and future system upgrades. Administrators should maintain a log of all sysctl changes, including the parameters adjusted, the rationale for the modification, and any observed impacts on system performance. This documentation can help ensure that the configuration is transparent and understandable to other administrators or teams who might need to maintain or audit the system in the future. This documentation also provides a point of reference for reverting changes if needed, and it is especially useful in multi-user environments where different administrators may be responsible for managing different aspects of system configuration.

Additionally, administrators should make sysctl optimizations persistent across reboots. While changes made via the sysctl -w command take effect immediately, they are not permanent unless explicitly saved. To make sysctl settings persistent, administrators should edit the /etc/sysctl.conf file or place configuration files in the /etc/sysctl.d/ directory. These files contain key-value pairs representing the desired kernel parameters, and they are automatically applied during the system's startup. By ensuring that sysctl settings are written to these files, administrators can guarantee that their optimizations persist after system reboots. It is also good practice to apply changes to the running system immediately using the sysctl -p or sysctl --system commands, which will reload the configuration files and apply the settings without requiring a reboot.

When optimizing sysctl settings, administrators should also take into account the system's hardware resources, such as CPU, memory, and network interfaces. In some cases, hardware limitations may impose constraints on how much optimization can be achieved. For example, a system with limited memory might not benefit from increased buffer sizes or low vm.swappiness values, as these settings could cause excessive swapping or resource exhaustion. Similarly, a system with a slow network interface may not see substantial performance improvements from adjusting TCP buffer settings. It is important to consider the system's resource capabilities and tailor optimizations accordingly.

Lastly, sysctl optimizations should be revisited periodically as system requirements and workloads evolve. Performance tuning is not a one-time task but an ongoing process. As new applications are deployed, system workloads change, or hardware upgrades are made, sysctl settings that were once ideal may no longer be the best fit. Administrators should periodically review and test their sysctl settings to ensure that the system continues to run optimally as it adapts to new demands.

Optimizing sysctl settings can greatly enhance the performance, stability, and security of a system, but it requires careful planning, testing, and documentation. By focusing on relevant parameters, testing changes incrementally, balancing performance with security, and ensuring persistence across reboots, administrators can fine-tune their systems for optimal efficiency. Sysctl provides a versatile and powerful tool for kernel-level tuning, and when used correctly, it allows administrators to manage system resources and behavior to meet the specific needs of any workload or environment.

Introduction to Daemons and Their Role

In UNIX-like operating systems, daemons play a crucial role in the overall operation of the system. These are background processes that run continuously, performing various tasks without direct user interaction. Daemons are essential for maintaining system functions and services, from managing network connections and handling file system operations to performing scheduled tasks and ensuring system security. Their role extends far beyond basic process management, as they help automate numerous processes that would otherwise require manual intervention, enabling systems to operate more efficiently and reliably.

The term "daemon" itself has its roots in the early days of computing. It is derived from the word "demon," which, in this context, refers to an entity that works quietly in the background, similar to how daemons operate without direct user involvement. Daemons are typically launched during system startup and continue running in the background throughout the system's uptime. They are designed to provide essential services, such as managing network requests, handling database queries, executing scheduled tasks, and maintaining system logs. Daemons are integral to ensuring that systems remain functional and responsive, even when users are not actively interacting with them.

One of the key characteristics of daemons is that they are independent of any user session. Unlike regular processes, which are started by users and run under the user's session, daemons typically run as system services and are independent of user login sessions. This allows daemons to provide services continuously, even when no user is logged in. For example, web servers, database servers, and print spoolers are all daemons that run in the background, awaiting incoming requests and processing them as needed. These processes are vital to the operation of many networked applications and services, and they need to be available at all times to ensure smooth system operations.

Daemons typically run with lower privileges than regular user processes to ensure system security and stability. While a regular user may have permission to start processes that run within their own session, daemons often run with restricted permissions to limit the potential damage caused by bugs or security vulnerabilities. For instance, a web server daemon might run with the least privileges required to serve web pages but would not have access to sensitive system files or the ability to make changes to other processes. This principle of least privilege is crucial for reducing the risk of system compromise and ensuring that daemons do not have unnecessary access to critical system resources.

Daemons can be divided into two broad categories based on their functionality: system daemons and user daemons. System daemons are responsible for performing essential tasks related to system management, such as process scheduling, logging, and network communication. For example, the cron daemon is responsible for executing scheduled tasks, such as backups or system maintenance, at specified times. The syslog daemon handles logging, capturing messages from the kernel and various applications to provide administrators with insights into system events and errors. Similarly, networking daemons like the SSH daemon (sshd) manage secure shell connections, while the Apache HTTP server daemon (httpd) listens for incoming web requests and serves web pages.

User daemons, on the other hand, are typically started by individual users to provide services specific to their needs. These daemons might be related to personal applications, such as file synchronization tools, chat servers, or media servers. While system daemons are often critical to system functionality and are started automatically at boot, user daemons are typically launched manually or as part of the user's session. They tend to be less essential to the system's overall operation but still play a vital role in enabling personalized or specialized services for users.

Daemons typically follow a well-defined lifecycle. They are initiated during the system's boot process, either by an init system or a service manager like systemd, and continue running until the system shuts down or the daemon is manually stopped. The init system, which is responsible for initializing the system during startup, often handles the starting of critical system daemons. For example, on systems using systemd, daemons are managed through unit files that specify how and when each service should start, restart, or stop. The init system monitors these processes to ensure that critical daemons are always running, automatically restarting them if they fail.

Once started, daemons run continuously, waiting for events or requests that trigger them to perform their tasks. For instance, a mail daemon waits for incoming emails, processes them, and then routes them to the correct recipients. Similarly, a database daemon waits for database queries and handles data storage and retrieval. Daemons often work in conjunction with other processes or daemons to perform complex tasks. For example, a network daemon might interact with a firewall daemon to ensure secure communication between different systems.

A critical aspect of daemon management is ensuring that they are configured and monitored appropriately. Daemons typically generate logs, which administrators can use to track their activity and diagnose any issues. These logs provide valuable information about the state of the daemon, any errors or issues it encounters, and how it is interacting with other system components. For example, the Apache HTTP server daemon logs incoming requests, errors, and performance data, which administrators can use to troubleshoot issues or monitor the health of the web server.

System administrators can also configure daemons to ensure that they run efficiently and securely. Configuration files for daemons often allow administrators to specify options like resource limits, security settings, and logging preferences. For example, a web server daemon might have configuration options to set the maximum number of concurrent connections, specify document root directories, or control how access is authenticated. These configurations help administrators fine-tune the behavior of daemons to meet the needs of the system or application.

In addition to being crucial for system operation, daemons also play a role in ensuring the system remains secure. Many daemons have specific security mechanisms in place to prevent unauthorized access or malicious activity. For example, SSH daemons are configured to accept only secure login credentials and typically limit login attempts to protect against brute force attacks. Similarly, the cron daemon allows administrators to automate security tasks, such as running security updates or checking for vulnerabilities on a regular schedule. Monitoring and securing daemons are vital to maintaining the integrity of the system and preventing attacks.

The role of daemons extends far beyond basic system processes. Daemons help automate system management tasks, enhance the functionality of the system, and provide continuous services to users and applications. Their background operation ensures that systems remain responsive, efficient, and secure, handling everything from scheduling tasks to managing network requests and monitoring system activity. As computing environments become more complex and interconnected, daemons will continue to play a central role in keeping systems running smoothly and securely, making them indispensable components of modern operating systems.

Managing System Daemons: Overview and Tools

System daemons are fundamental to the operation of UNIX-like operating systems. They are background processes that perform a wide variety of essential tasks, ranging from managing system resources to providing services such as networking, logging, and scheduled task execution. Daemons are vital for the ongoing, uninterrupted functioning of the system, running without direct user intervention. These processes are often initiated at system boot and remain active until the system is shut down. Their management is crucial for maintaining system stability, ensuring services run smoothly, and securing the environment. Understanding how to manage these daemons and the tools available for their administration is critical for system administrators.

Daemons are typically designed to run in the background and operate independently of user sessions. They provide services that do not require direct interaction from the user but are essential for the system's operation. For instance, a print server daemon might continuously listen for print jobs sent from other machines on the network, while a web server daemon waits for incoming HTTP requests to serve web pages. Many daemons are related to specific system functionalities, such as logging, networking, or hardware management. These daemons ensure that processes such as log management, email delivery, and system health monitoring occur without interruption. Most daemons are designed to start automatically during system boot and continue running until the system is powered off, offering a seamless and persistent service to users and other processes.

The management of system daemons involves starting, stopping, restarting, and configuring them as necessary. Unlike user applications, daemons typically do not interact directly with the user. Instead, they operate in the background, responding to system events or external requests. System administrators have the responsibility of configuring daemons to meet the needs of the system and its users, as well as ensuring they are running optimally. In addition, daemons often require monitoring to ensure they are functioning correctly and not consuming excessive resources or encountering errors.

One of the most important tools for managing system daemons is the init system. The init system is responsible for managing the system's startup and shutdown processes. It is the first process that runs when the system boots and is responsible for starting other processes, including daemons. On many UNIX-like systems, the traditional init system is known as SysVinit. However, modern systems typically use more advanced init systems such as systemd, which provides greater flexibility and control over service management. Systemd has become the standard init system for many Linux distributions, offering enhanced functionality such as parallel service startup, dependency management, and improved logging.

Systemd provides administrators with powerful tools for managing system daemons. The systemctl command is used to start, stop, restart, enable, and disable services (daemons). For example, to start a service, an administrator would run systemctl start <service_name>, where <service_name> is the name of the daemon. Similarly, to stop a running service, the systemctl stop <service_name> command can be used. For services that should start automatically during boot, administrators can enable them using the systemctl enable <service_name> command. Conversely, to prevent a service from starting automatically, the systemctl disable <service_name> command is used. The systemctl status <service_name> command provides information about the status of a service, including whether it is running, its PID (process ID), and any recent logs associated with the service.

Systemd also supports the management of service dependencies, allowing administrators to configure daemons to start in a specific order based on their relationships with other services. This ensures that critical services are started first and that dependent services are launched afterward. For example, a web server daemon may depend on a database daemon being available, so the systemd configuration ensures the database daemon is started before the web server. This level of control is essential for complex systems that rely on multiple interconnected services to function properly.

For systems using SysVinit, the service command is used to manage daemons. The service <service_name> start command starts the specified daemon, while service <service_name> stop will stop it. SysVinit is less flexible than systemd, but it is still widely used in older systems or in systems that prioritize simplicity over the advanced features provided by systemd.

Another critical tool for managing system daemons is ps, which is used to view running processes, including daemons. By running ps aux, administrators can see all processes running on the system, including daemons. This command displays essential information about each process, such as its PID, memory usage, CPU time, and command line arguments. Administrators can use this information to identify processes that are consuming excessive resources or to track down unresponsive daemons.

In addition to ps, administrators can use top or htop to monitor system processes in real-time. These tools provide dynamic views of system activity, allowing administrators to see which processes are consuming the most resources. htop is an enhanced version of top, offering a more user-friendly interface and additional features like process tree views and easier navigation. These tools are valuable for identifying system bottlenecks, monitoring resource usage, and troubleshooting daemon performance issues.

When managing system daemons, administrators also need to configure them properly to meet specific system requirements. Daemons often have configuration files that allow administrators to adjust their behavior, such as setting network parameters, file paths, or authentication settings. For example, the Apache web server daemon has a configuration file that defines the web server's document root, logging settings, and allowed network connections. Modifying these configuration files enables administrators to customize the behavior of daemons to fit the needs of the system or the application they are supporting.

Security is also an essential aspect of managing daemons. Many daemons run with high privileges, and a compromised daemon could lead to system exploitation. To mitigate these risks, administrators should configure daemons to run with the least privileges necessary for their function. For example, many daemons, such as the SSH daemon (sshd), allow administrators to restrict which users can access the system and what actions they are permitted to perform. Similarly, some daemons provide options to limit their access to specific resources, such as restricting file access or network ports.

To ensure that daemons continue to run smoothly, administrators must also monitor their activity regularly. System logs, which are typically generated by the syslog daemon, contain valuable information about the performance of daemons and any issues they encounter. Logs can help identify errors, warnings, or performance bottlenecks that may affect the operation of daemons. Administrators should regularly review these logs to ensure that daemons are functioning as expected and troubleshoot any issues that arise.

Managing system daemons is a crucial aspect of system administration. Daemons provide essential services that allow systems to operate continuously without direct user intervention. Whether using systemd, SysVinit, or other tools, administrators must be familiar with the tools and techniques for starting, stopping, and configuring daemons. Through effective management and monitoring, system administrators can ensure that these background processes continue to operate efficiently and securely, providing critical services to both users and applications.

Controlling Daemons with Systemd

Systemd is the default initialization system and service manager on many modern Linux distributions. It is responsible for booting the system, managing processes, and controlling system services, including daemons. Daemons are essential for background tasks, system processes, and various services that need to run continuously without direct user interaction. They range from network services, such as web servers and database services, to system maintenance tasks, like log management and resource monitoring. Systemd provides administrators with a robust set of tools to control and manage these daemons, ensuring that they run correctly, restart when necessary, and provide the necessary services for a functional system.

At the core of Systemd is the concept of service units, which are configuration files that define how system services should behave. Daemons are essentially system services managed by systemd, and each daemon is associated with a corresponding unit file. These unit files specify how and when a daemon should be started, stopped, or restarted. They also define important properties, such as dependencies on other services, resource limits, and logging configurations. Understanding how to work with these unit files is critical for effectively controlling daemons with Systemd.

The most common way to manage system daemons with systemd is by using the systemctl command. This command provides a wide range of options for interacting with systemd, allowing administrators to start, stop, restart, enable, disable, and view the status of services. When managing daemons, administrators can use systemctl to check the current status of a service, start it if it is not running, stop it if it is no longer needed, or restart it if a configuration change has been made. For example, to start a daemon, an administrator would use systemctl start <service_name>, where <service_name> is the name of the service's unit file, such as systemctl start apache2 to start the Apache web server daemon. Similarly, to stop a running service, the command systemctl stop <service_name> is used.

A key aspect of controlling daemons with systemd is the ability to enable or disable them to start automatically at boot. This is particularly useful for ensuring that critical daemons are always running when the system starts. For example, a web server or database service may need to be available as soon as the system is up. Administrators can enable a service to start automatically with the systemctl enable <service_name> command. This command creates symbolic links that tell systemd to start the daemon at boot. Conversely, if a service should not start automatically, the systemctl disable <service_name> command will prevent it from being launched at boot time.

In addition to starting and stopping daemons, administrators often need to restart them, especially when changes are made to their configuration files. The systemctl restart <service_name> command allows administrators to restart a daemon, which is useful when a configuration change requires the daemon to reload its settings without rebooting the entire system. This ensures that any updates to configuration files take effect immediately. Similarly, the systemctl reload <service_name> command can be used to reload the service's configuration without stopping and restarting it entirely, which is useful for services that support graceful reloading, such as web servers.

Systemd also provides a powerful feature for monitoring the status of daemons. The systemctl status <service_name> command allows administrators to view detailed information about the current state of a service, including whether it is active, inactive, or failed. This command also shows the process ID (PID) of the running service, memory and CPU usage, and recent log entries related to the service. This is valuable for troubleshooting and ensuring that daemons are functioning as expected. If a daemon fails to start or encounters an error, the output from systemctl status can provide helpful clues about the cause of the problem, such as configuration errors or missing dependencies.

Another important feature of systemd is its ability to handle service dependencies. Some daemons depend on other services being available before they can start. For example, a web server may require a database daemon to be running before it can serve content. Systemd allows administrators to define service dependencies in the unit files using directives like Requires, Wants, Before, and After. These directives define the order in which services are started or stopped. For instance, the After directive ensures that one service is started only after another service has been successfully launched. This allows administrators to control the startup sequence and avoid issues with services failing due to unmet dependencies.

In addition to managing the start and stop of daemons, systemd also provides features for handling service failures. Daemons may encounter errors or unexpected crashes, and systemd offers automatic restart functionality to keep services running. The Restart directive in a service's unit file defines the conditions under which the service should be restarted. For example, setting Restart=on-failure ensures that a service is automatically restarted if it exits with a non-zero exit code, indicating an error. Administrators can configure systemd to attempt to restart a service a specific number of times or indefinitely, providing fault tolerance and minimizing downtime for critical services.

For administrators who want to automate their management of daemons, systemd offers timers, which are used to schedule and execute tasks automatically, similar to cron jobs but with more integration into the systemd ecosystem. Systemd timers allow administrators to run services at specific intervals, for example, to perform system maintenance tasks, backup operations, or cleanup jobs. Timers are defined using unit files that are similar to service files but include time-based directives instead of process management details. By using timers, administrators can leverage the full capabilities of systemd to schedule and manage background tasks, all while ensuring that they are tightly integrated with the system's overall service management.

In addition to the core service management functionality, systemd also supports advanced logging features through the journal. The journalctl command allows administrators to access the logs for system services, including those managed by systemd. This can be crucial for diagnosing issues with daemons, especially when they fail to start or encounter unexpected behavior. The logs are stored in a binary format and are highly structured, allowing administrators to query them efficiently. For example, journalctl -u <service_name> will show logs specific to a given service, making it easier to troubleshoot problems.

Systemd provides a centralized and consistent way to manage daemons across different Linux distributions. By standardizing service management, systemd makes it easier for administrators to handle the lifecycle of daemons, automate tasks, and improve system stability and performance. Whether starting or stopping services, managing dependencies, configuring automatic restarts, or troubleshooting failures, systemd provides the tools necessary to ensure that daemons function as expected, contributing to the smooth and secure operation of the system. By mastering systemd, administrators can gain full control over system services, optimize performance, and improve system reliability.

Configuring Daemons for Automatic Startup

In any operating system, particularly in UNIX-like systems, daemons play a critical role in providing essential services that keep the system running smoothly. These background processes ensure that various tasks, such as network communication, system monitoring, logging, and resource management, are handled without direct user intervention. Configuring daemons to start automatically when the system boots up is essential for maintaining system stability and ensuring that key services are always available. This process allows administrators to reduce manual intervention and automate system management, making systems more reliable and easier to maintain. In this chapter, we will explore how to configure daemons for automatic startup, ensuring that essential services are always running when the system is rebooted.

Automatic startup of daemons is typically managed by the system's init system, which is responsible for booting the operating system and managing system services. In modern Linux distributions, systemd has become the default init system, replacing older systems like SysVinit. Systemd provides robust tools for managing daemons and their automatic startup, giving administrators fine-grained control over which services start at boot, in what order, and under what conditions. Understanding how to configure daemons for automatic startup with systemd is an essential skill for system administrators.

To configure a daemon for automatic startup, administrators typically use systemd unit files. These unit files contain the configuration settings for system services and daemons, defining their behavior, dependencies, resource limits, and start conditions. Unit files are typically located in the /etc/systemd/system/ directory or in directories like /lib/systemd/system/, depending on the system and the specific service. Each unit file defines how and when the daemon should be started, whether it should be restarted if it fails, and what other services it depends on.

One of the key aspects of configuring automatic startup for a daemon is ensuring that it is enabled to start during boot. This is achieved using the systemctl enable command, which creates symbolic links between the unit file and the appropriate directories, instructing systemd to start the service during the boot process. For instance, if an administrator wants to configure the Apache web server daemon (apache2) to start automatically at boot, they would use the command systemctl enable apache2.service. This command enables the service and ensures that it will be started whenever the system is rebooted. The systemctl enable command essentially tells systemd to link the service's unit file to the system's default runlevel, so it starts up when the system boots.

Once a daemon has been enabled for automatic startup, administrators can verify its status using the systemctl is-enabled command. For example, running systemctl is-enabled apache2.service will confirm whether Apache is set to start automatically at boot. If the service is enabled, the output will indicate "enabled," while if it is not set to start automatically, the output will indicate "disabled." This is useful for administrators to check and confirm that the correct services are enabled for automatic startup.

Systemd also allows administrators to control the order in which daemons are started during boot. This is important because some services rely on other services being available before they can be started. For instance, a web server daemon might require a database daemon to be running before it can serve content. Systemd provides mechanisms like the After, Before, Requires, and Wants directives in unit files to define dependencies between services. For example, a web server unit file might include the directive After=network.target, which ensures that the network service is started before the web server. Similarly, the Requires directive can be used to specify that one service must be running before another can start. By carefully configuring these dependencies, administrators can ensure that services are started in the correct order, avoiding errors and ensuring the system runs efficiently.

In some cases, administrators may need to adjust the default startup behavior of daemons based on specific conditions. Systemd provides various directives in the unit files to control how services are started, restarted, and stopped. For instance, the Restart directive controls whether a daemon should be restarted automatically if it fails. This is particularly useful for critical services that need to remain running at all times. By setting Restart=always in the unit file, systemd will automatically restart the service whenever it crashes or stops unexpectedly. Other values, such as on-failure, ensure that the service is only restarted when it exits with an error, while no disables automatic restarts.

In addition to controlling when daemons start, administrators can also configure them to be started on demand, rather than at boot. This is useful for services that may not be needed immediately but are required later on. Systemd supports on-demand services using socket activation, which means that a service can be started when it receives a request, such as a network connection. Socket-based activation allows for more efficient use of system resources, as services are only started when they are actually needed. For example, the sshd daemon may be configured to start only when an SSH connection is requested, rather than starting automatically during boot.

Configuring daemons for automatic startup also involves ensuring that they are properly managed and monitored once they are running. Systemd offers several tools for monitoring and controlling daemons after they have been started. The systemctl status <service_name> command provides real-time information about the daemon's status, including whether it is active, inactive, or failed. If a service encounters an issue or fails to start, administrators can use this information to troubleshoot the problem. Systemd also integrates with the system journal, providing detailed logs of service activity, errors, and warnings. Using the journalctl command, administrators can view logs related to specific services, allowing them to identify issues and take corrective action.

In some cases, administrators may need to configure certain daemons to start automatically only under specific conditions. For instance, a daemon may be required to start only when a particular hardware device is connected or when certain network conditions are met. Systemd allows for advanced configuration using conditions such as ConditionPathExists, ConditionKernelVersion, and ConditionHost. These conditions allow for more granular control over when a daemon should start, based on system state or configuration. This level of flexibility is especially useful in complex environments with varying requirements.

Once daemons are configured for automatic startup, administrators should regularly review and test the configurations to ensure that the system is functioning as intended. Over time, system requirements may change, and daemons may need to be added, removed, or reconfigured. By using systemd's tools for managing service units, administrators can maintain a well-organized and efficient system where critical services are always available and running as expected.

Configuring daemons for automatic startup with systemd is essential for maintaining a reliable and efficient system. By using the appropriate tools and understanding how to define service dependencies, adjust service startup behavior, and monitor the health of daemons, administrators can ensure that the system remains responsive and functional at all times. Whether for managing basic services or handling complex, dependent service chains, systemd provides a comprehensive and powerful method for controlling and automating the startup of daemons, allowing administrators to ensure that critical services are available when needed.

Daemon Logging and Monitoring

Daemons are essential components of any UNIX-like operating system, providing background services that ensure the system runs smoothly. From handling networking requests to managing system logs, daemons play a vital role in the operation of a server or workstation. However, because daemons typically run in the background and are not directly interacted with by users, it is essential to monitor their activity and collect logs to ensure they are functioning as expected. Proper logging and monitoring of daemons are crucial for detecting issues early, diagnosing problems, and ensuring system stability and security. This chapter will explore how daemons handle logging, how administrators can monitor their performance, and the tools available to help manage daemon logs effectively.

Logging is a critical aspect of daemon management because it allows administrators to capture detailed information about the system's activities, service operations, and potential issues. Without proper logging, identifying the cause of a failure or determining the health of a service can be extremely difficult. Fortunately, UNIX-like systems provide robust logging mechanisms, allowing daemons to output logs that track their actions and report any errors. By default, many daemons use system logging services, such as syslog or the systemd journal, to record important events, errors, and warnings related to their operations.

Syslog is one of the oldest and most widely used logging systems for UNIX-like systems. It allows daemons to send log messages to a central logging service, which stores the messages in log files such as /var/log/syslog or /var/log/messages. Daemons communicate with syslog by writing log entries to a specified log facility and severity level. For example, the Apache HTTP server daemon may write messages about incoming requests, errors, or warnings to the syslog service, which then stores these messages in log files. The syslog service organizes the log messages based on the configured facilities (such as daemon, auth, or localo) and their severity levels (such as info, error, or warning).

Syslog is flexible and allows for the configuration of different log levels, so administrators can capture varying amounts of detail depending on the needs of the system. For example, an administrator may configure a daemon to only log critical errors during normal operation, while enabling more verbose logging (e.g., debug level) during troubleshooting or when performing system audits. By adjusting the logging configuration, administrators can tailor the amount of information recorded, balancing between capturing necessary details and avoiding overwhelming the system with excessive log data.

In modern Linux distributions, systemd has largely replaced syslog, introducing its own logging system known as the journal. The systemd journal offers several advantages over traditional syslog logging, particularly in terms of performance, structure, and integration with other system services. Unlike syslog, which stores logs as plain text files, systemd journal stores logs in a binary format, allowing for faster searching, filtering, and indexing. This makes it easier for administrators to retrieve specific log entries or search for patterns across large datasets.

Daemons that are managed by systemd typically log their output directly to the journal. The journal captures logs not only from daemons but also from the kernel, system services, and user applications. This centralization of logs ensures that administrators can easily monitor system activity and troubleshoot issues across all aspects of the system. To view the logs of a specific daemon, administrators can use the journalctl command, which allows for flexible querying of log data. For example, running journalctl -u

<service_name> will display the logs related to a specific daemon, making it easier to pinpoint errors or warnings related to that service.

The journalctl command provides powerful filtering and searching options, allowing administrators to narrow down the logs by time, priority level, or specific messages. For example, administrators can use journalctl -p err to display only the error messages, or journalctl --since "1 hour ago" to view logs from the past hour. The ability to filter logs in real time makes it much easier to identify issues and respond to potential system failures quickly.

While syslog and the systemd journal are commonly used for logging daemon activity, daemons themselves may also have their own logging mechanisms. Many daemons are configured with their own log files, allowing them to log information directly to a specific location. For example, the Apache web server daemon typically logs HTTP requests, errors, and performance metrics to a file located at /var/log/apache2/access.log or /var/log/apache2/error.log. Similarly, database daemons like MySQL or PostgreSQL store logs related to queries, connections, and errors in their respective log files.

To effectively monitor these logs, administrators can use log management tools that centralize, organize, and analyze log data from different sources. Tools like logrotate are commonly used to manage log file sizes, rotating them periodically to prevent log files from consuming excessive disk space. By configuring logrotate, administrators can set limits on log file sizes, define how many backup copies of logs to keep, and specify how frequently logs should be rotated. This ensures that log files remain manageable while preserving important historical data for auditing and troubleshooting purposes.

For more advanced monitoring of daemon performance, administrators can use specialized tools that provide real-time analysis of system activity. For instance, tools like top, htop, and atop offer real-time monitoring of CPU, memory, and process usage, allowing administrators to identify resource bottlenecks or performance issues with specific daemons. These tools allow administrators to drill down into the system's resource consumption, helping them diagnose problems like high CPU usage or excessive memory consumption caused by a misbehaving daemon.

In addition to these traditional monitoring tools, modern systems often use integrated monitoring solutions like Prometheus, Nagios, or Zabbix to track daemon performance and system health over time. These monitoring systems gather metrics from daemons, log data, and system resources, presenting the information in user-friendly dashboards. By setting up alerts for certain thresholds, administrators can be notified in real time about potential issues, such as when a daemon fails, a system resource is overused, or a service becomes unresponsive.

System logs also play a crucial role in system security. Daemons, especially those involved in network services, often generate logs related to access attempts, authentication failures, and other security-related events. By monitoring these logs, administrators can detect unauthorized access attempts, brute force attacks, or other suspicious activity. Many daemons are configured to log failed login attempts, connection attempts from unknown IP addresses, or changes to system configurations, which can be invaluable for identifying and mitigating security threats.

Daemon logging and monitoring are vital for maintaining the health, performance, and security of UNIX-like systems. By utilizing the right tools and configuring daemons to log essential information, administrators can ensure that services are operating correctly and can quickly address any issues that arise. Regularly reviewing and analyzing daemon logs is an essential part of system administration, allowing for proactive monitoring and timely intervention when problems are detected. Whether using traditional logging systems like syslog or modern solutions like systemd journal and integrated monitoring tools, administrators have a variety of powerful resources to manage and track daemon activity, ensuring systems run smoothly and securely.

Debugging Daemons with Journalctl

In UNIX-like operating systems, daemons are critical background processes that provide essential services to users and applications. These daemons often run without direct interaction from the user, making it difficult to track their status or diagnose issues when something goes wrong. This is where logging becomes essential. Logs provide valuable information about the operation of daemons, capturing events, errors, warnings, and other messages that are crucial for debugging and troubleshooting. One of the most powerful tools for managing and analyzing logs in modern Linux systems is journalctl, a command-line utility that interacts with the systemd journal to retrieve and display log entries. Understanding how to effectively use journalctl to debug daemons is essential for system administrators who need to ensure that their services are running smoothly and reliably.

Systemd, the init system used by many modern Linux distributions, integrates a comprehensive logging mechanism called the journal. Unlike traditional syslog-based logging systems, the systemd journal stores log messages in a binary format, offering several advantages such as fast searching, more structured data, and the ability to correlate log entries across different services. The journal captures logs not only from system daemons but also from the kernel, user applications, and system services, providing a centralized and powerful logging solution. Since daemons managed by systemd log their output to the journal, journalctl becomes the go-to tool for querying, analyzing, and debugging daemon logs.

When debugging a daemon, the first step is to access the logs relevant to the specific service. To do this, administrators use the journalctl command with the -u option, followed by the name of the service unit. For example, to view the logs of the Apache HTTP server daemon, an administrator would run journalctl -u apache2.service. This command filters the log entries, displaying only those related to the specified daemon. By examining these log entries, administrators can identify errors, warnings, and other messages that may provide insight into the daemon's behavior.

One of the most useful features of journalctl is its ability to display logs in real-time, allowing administrators to monitor a daemon's activity as it happens. The -f option, similar to the tail -f command, allows administrators to view log entries as they are written to the journal. For example, journalctl -u apache2.service -f will show the real-time output of the Apache daemon, updating automatically as new log messages are generated. This can be especially useful when investigating a daemon's performance during an issue or when troubleshooting problems that are occurring in real time.

In addition to filtering logs by service, journalctl provides several other powerful options for narrowing down search results. For example, administrators can use the --since and --until options to specify a time range for the logs they wish to view. For instance, journalctl -u apache2.service --since "2022-04-01" --until "2022-04-02" will display only the logs generated by Apache between April 1st and April 2nd of 2022. These time-based filters are useful when administrators need to isolate log entries for a specific event or error that occurred within a defined time window. Additionally, administrators can use the -p option to filter log entries by priority level, such as journalctl -p err to view only error messages or journalctl -p warning to see warning-level logs.

When debugging a daemon, it is essential to understand not only what the daemon is doing but also why it might be failing. journalctl can help reveal the root cause of issues by providing context, including detailed error messages, stack traces, and resource utilization information. For example, when a daemon crashes or encounters an issue, the log entries may include error codes, memory allocation problems, or missing configuration files. By reviewing these entries, administrators can trace the issue back to its source, whether it is an incorrect configuration, a resource limitation, or a conflict with other services.

Systemd's journal is designed to store logs in a binary format, which offers several advantages over traditional text-based logging systems. However, it also means that administrators cannot simply open the log files in a text editor. Instead, journalctl provides a structured way to query and view the logs in a human-readable format. Administrators can view logs as they are written or query historical logs, making it easier to troubleshoot issues that may have occurred long after the problem arose. In fact, the journal has several built-in features that enhance its ability to help administrators debug daemons, such as the ability to filter logs based on a service's PID or the ability to view logs from a specific boot session using the -b option.

Beyond basic log inspection, journalctl also supports advanced filtering options that allow administrators to drill down into the logs for more detailed debugging. For example, administrators can filter logs by specific fields, such as the message content, PID, or unit name, allowing for more targeted searches. To search for logs that contain a particular string or pattern, administrators can use the grep utility in combination with journalctl. For instance, running journalctl -u apache2.service | grep "error" will display only the error messages related to Apache, making it easier to focus on specific issues. This ability to perform advanced searches within daemon logs is invaluable for isolating problems and quickly identifying potential solutions.

In many cases, daemons log both informational messages and errors, and identifying the severity of the issue is essential when troubleshooting. journalctl provides various log levels, such as info, warning, err, and critical, that indicate the severity of log messages. When debugging a daemon, it is helpful to focus on error messages (err or critical) first, as these are likely to indicate the source of the problem. Administrators can use the -p option with journalctl to filter logs by these levels. For example, using journalctl -p err -u apache2.service will display only error messages related to Apache, allowing the administrator to quickly focus on critical issues.

Another useful feature for debugging daemons is the ability to check logs from previous boot sessions. When troubleshooting persistent problems, administrators may need to view logs from a specific boot or from when the system last started. The -b option with journalctl allows administrators to view logs from the current or previous boot session. For example, running journalctl -b -1 will show logs from the previous boot, which can be useful when diagnosing issues that arose after the system was restarted. This option is especially beneficial when debugging problems that may not be immediately apparent but only occur during specific boot sequences.

Debugging daemons using journalctl provides administrators with the tools to troubleshoot issues efficiently. By offering a structured, searchable, and real-time interface for system logs, journalctl enables administrators to quickly identify errors, track service failures, and gather insights into daemon behavior. As daemon management becomes increasingly important in modern computing, mastering tools like journalctl is crucial for maintaining system health, ensuring service availability, and preventing downtime caused by daemon failures. By utilizing the full capabilities of journalctl, administrators can perform effective and thorough debugging, ensuring that daemons run optimally and continue to provide critical services to users and applications.

Writing Custom Daemons: A Beginner's Guide

Daemons are a cornerstone of UNIX-like operating systems, providing essential background services that keep the system running smoothly. These processes run without user interaction, handling tasks such as managing network connections, performing system maintenance, and running scheduled jobs. While many daemons are pre-installed and managed by the system, there are times when creating custom daemons is necessary. Whether for automating tasks, integrating services, or developing new features, writing custom daemons is a valuable skill for system administrators and developers. This chapter introduces the process of writing custom daemons from a beginner's perspective, covering the fundamentals of daemon creation, best practices, and how to integrate them into the system for efficient operation.

A daemon is a type of process that runs in the background and typically performs tasks that are independent of user interactions. It often runs continuously from the time the system starts up until it is shut down. Unlike regular processes, which run in the context of a user session, daemons usually do not have an associated terminal or user interface. They are essential for the operation of many system services, such as web servers, database servers, and logging systems, which require continuous operation without interruption.

To write a custom daemon, it is important to first understand how daemons work within the system. A daemon typically starts as a regular process that detaches itself from the terminal and runs in the background. This detachment involves creating a new session, which ensures that the daemon is not tied to a specific user's terminal and can continue running even if the user logs out. In Linux systems, this is usually accomplished by calling fork() to create a child process, followed by setsid() to start a new session and detach from the controlling terminal. These system calls ensure that the daemon is independent and can continue running without user intervention.

Once the daemon process is created and detached, it typically needs to perform a specific task, such as monitoring a file, handling network requests, or processing data in the background. The core functionality of the daemon is implemented in a loop, which continues to run as long as the daemon is active. This loop can be designed to handle specific events, such as listening for incoming network connections or checking the status of a particular resource. The key is that the daemon runs continuously and only stops when it is explicitly terminated or when the system shuts down.

For example, a simple daemon might be written in Python to monitor a directory for changes. The daemon would run in a loop, periodically checking the contents of the directory for new or modified files. If a change is detected, it could perform a predefined action, such as sending a notification or processing the file. This basic structure is the foundation for most daemons, where the main difference lies in the tasks they perform and how they interact with other system services.

In addition to basic functionality, daemons must handle certain housekeeping tasks to ensure they run efficiently and securely. One important consideration is logging. Since daemons run in the background, it is essential to capture relevant information about their operation for troubleshooting and auditing purposes. This can be done by redirecting the output of the daemon to log files or using a system logging service like syslog or the systemd journal. By capturing logs, administrators and developers can track the daemon's activity, detect errors, and improve system performance.

Another important aspect of writing custom daemons is handling signal processing. Daemons often need to respond to external signals to control their behavior. For instance, they may need to reload configuration files, gracefully shut down, or restart when certain conditions are met. In UNIX-like systems, signals such as SIGTERM (terminate), SIGHUP (hang-up), and SIGINT (interrupt) are used to control the behavior of processes. A custom daemon should be designed to handle these signals appropriately, allowing it to clean up resources, save state, or reconfigure itself as needed. For example, a daemon could listen for the SIGHUP signal to reload its configuration file without requiring a restart.

Once the daemon's functionality is in place, it is essential to ensure that it can be integrated with the system's service management framework for automatic startup and monitoring. On modern Linux systems, systemd is the most commonly used service manager, providing a powerful mechanism for managing background processes and daemons. To integrate a custom daemon with systemd, administrators create a unit file that defines how the daemon should be started, stopped, and monitored. This unit file specifies details such as the daemon's executable path, dependencies on other services, resource limits, and whether the daemon should automatically restart if it fails.

For example, a basic systemd unit file for a custom daemon might look like this:

[Unit]

Description=My Custom Daemon

After=network.target

[Service]

ExecStart=/usr/bin/my_custom_daemon

Restart=on-failure

[Install]

WantedBy=multi-user.target

In this example, the ExecStart directive specifies the path to the custom daemon's executable, while the Restart=on-failure directive ensures that the daemon will be automatically restarted if it crashes. The [Install] section defines that the daemon should be started during the system boot process by associating it with the multi-user.target, which is a typical runlevel for system services.

Once the unit file is created, administrators can use the systemctl command to enable, start, and manage the custom daemon. By running systemctl enable my_custom_daemon.service, administrators can ensure that the daemon will start automatically when the system boots. The systemctl start my_custom_daemon.service command starts the daemon immediately, while systemctl status my_custom_daemon.service allows administrators to check its status.

Creating custom daemons also requires considering resource usage and performance. Since daemons often run continuously, it is important to optimize them for minimal resource consumption. This can include optimizing memory usage, reducing CPU load, and ensuring that the daemon's operations do not interfere with other system processes. Additionally, daemons should be designed with scalability in mind, especially when they are responsible for handling a large number of requests or processing large amounts of data. Efficient algorithms and resource management techniques are crucial to ensuring that custom daemons remain responsive and do not degrade system performance over time.

Security is another crucial consideration when writing custom daemons. Daemons often have elevated privileges and can access sensitive system resources, making them potential targets for attackers. To reduce the risk of exploitation, custom daemons should follow the principle of least privilege, running with only the permissions necessary for their tasks. In addition, they should be designed to sanitize inputs, avoid race conditions, and ensure secure communication with other services. Security auditing tools can help identify vulnerabilities in the daemon's code and configuration, ensuring that it remains secure and resilient to attacks.

Writing custom daemons is an invaluable skill for system administrators and developers, allowing them to automate tasks, integrate services, and create specialized system processes. By understanding the principles of daemon creation, logging, monitoring, and integration with system services like systemd, administrators can ensure that their custom daemons are robust, efficient, and secure. Through careful design and consideration of system resources, security, and performance, custom daemons can significantly enhance the functionality of UNIX-like systems, providing background services that run smoothly and reliably.

Daemon Security: Securing the Running Services

Daemons are essential background processes that provide necessary services on UNIX-like systems. They handle a range of tasks, from managing network connections and running scheduled jobs to controlling hardware and system resources. However, since daemons often run with elevated privileges and manage sensitive system resources, they can also be a target for attackers if not properly secured. Ensuring that daemons are secure is crucial for maintaining the overall integrity, availability, and confidentiality of a system. This chapter focuses on securing running daemons, emphasizing key principles, best practices, and security strategies to protect these background services from unauthorized access and exploitation.

The first step in securing daemons is to understand their privileges and the resources they access. Many daemons run with root privileges, meaning they have unrestricted access to the system. This makes them attractive targets for attackers who might exploit vulnerabilities in the daemon to escalate their privileges and gain control of the system. To minimize the risks associated with running daemons with high privileges, it is essential to adhere to the principle of least privilege. This principle states that daemons should run with the minimum privileges necessary to perform their tasks. By configuring daemons to run under dedicated, non-privileged user accounts, administrators can limit the potential damage if an attacker successfully compromises the daemon.

When configuring a daemon to run with limited privileges, administrators should ensure that the associated user account has only the necessary permissions. For example, a web server daemon may not need access to the entire file system, so it should be configured to run with restricted permissions, only allowing access to the directories and files it needs to serve content. This reduces the impact of a potential security breach and limits the attack surface. In addition, some systems allow administrators to configure additional security features, such as process sandboxing, to further isolate daemons from each other and the rest of the system. Sandboxing ensures that even if a daemon is compromised, it cannot easily affect other services or the system as a whole.

Another critical aspect of securing daemons is ensuring that their communications are encrypted and authenticated. Many daemons communicate over networks, making them vulnerable to interception and man-in-the-middle attacks. Secure communication protocols, such as SSL/TLS, should be used to encrypt data in transit, ensuring that sensitive information is protected from unauthorized access. For example, a web server daemon should be configured to use HTTPS instead of HTTP to secure web traffic. Additionally, daemons that require remote management should use secure protocols like SSH, which provide strong encryption and authentication mechanisms. By enforcing the use of secure communication protocols, administrators can significantly reduce the risk of data theft or tampering.

Daemons often listen for incoming network connections, and exposing these services to the internet can increase the risk of attack. One effective strategy for securing daemons is to limit which IP addresses or networks can access specific services. This can be done using firewalls or network security policies to restrict incoming connections to trusted sources. For example, a database daemon might be configured to only allow connections from specific internal servers rather than from any external host. This greatly reduces the exposure of the service and helps protect against unauthorized access. In addition, administrators should regularly audit network services and close any unused or unnecessary ports to minimize the attack surface.

Another essential security measure for daemons is to keep them updated with the latest security patches. Daemon software, like any other software, can have vulnerabilities that, if left unpatched, can be exploited by attackers. Administrators should regularly check for updates and ensure that all daemons are running the latest stable versions, which include security fixes. In many cases, package managers or system management tools provide mechanisms for automatically applying security updates, ensuring that daemons remain secure without requiring constant manual intervention. In addition to applying updates, administrators should monitor security advisories for the specific daemons they are running to stay informed about known vulnerabilities and recommended mitigations.

Monitoring and logging are critical components of daemon security. Daemons should be configured to log their activity, including error messages, access logs, and security events. These logs provide valuable insights into the daemon's behavior and can help administrators identify abnormal activity or potential security breaches. For example, a web server daemon might log incoming requests, while a database daemon might log failed authentication attempts. By regularly reviewing these logs, administrators can detect signs of malicious activity, such as brute-force login attempts, and take appropriate action. Furthermore, log files should be protected from unauthorized access and tampering, as attackers could modify logs to cover their tracks. Administrators can enforce strict file permissions on log files and use log management tools to monitor and analyze them in real-time.

To enhance daemon security, administrators should also configure the daemon to handle error conditions safely. Many daemons have the ability to handle unexpected events, such as resource exhaustion, network failures, or configuration errors. In such cases, daemons should fail gracefully, without exposing sensitive information or leaving the system in an unstable state. For example, if a daemon encounters an error while processing a request, it should log the error and continue running, rather than crashing or exposing internal data. This helps ensure the availability of the service and reduces the potential attack surface created by error conditions. Administrators should also configure daemons to restart automatically if they crash, ensuring minimal disruption to service availability.

Furthermore, administrators should regularly perform security audits and vulnerability assessments on daemons. This can involve scanning for known security vulnerabilities using tools such as OpenVAS or

Nessus, as well as performing manual checks for misconfigurations or weak security settings. Regular audits help ensure that daemons are running with secure configurations and that any potential vulnerabilities are identified and addressed before they can be exploited. Security tools can also help identify outdated or unsupported daemons that may need to be replaced or patched.

In addition to auditing and monitoring, administrators should be prepared to respond to security incidents involving daemons. Having an incident response plan in place ensures that if a daemon is compromised, the administrator can quickly assess the damage, contain the attack, and restore normal operations. This plan should include steps for isolating affected services, gathering evidence, analyzing logs, and recovering from the attack. Administrators should also maintain backups of critical configurations and data, which can be used to restore services to a secure state if necessary.

Securing daemons is a multifaceted process that involves limiting privileges, securing communications, managing access, and ensuring regular updates and monitoring. By adhering to best practices, such as using secure communication protocols, limiting access to trusted sources, and monitoring daemon activity, administrators can significantly reduce the risks associated with running daemons on their systems. Effective daemon security requires ongoing vigilance, proactive management, and timely responses to emerging threats, but with the right tools and strategies in place, administrators can ensure that their systems remain secure and resilient against attack.

Daemons in Distributed Systems

In distributed systems, daemons play a pivotal role in managing the communication, coordination, and execution of tasks across multiple machines. A distributed system is a collection of independent entities that work together to achieve a common goal. These systems can be spread across multiple servers, data centers, or geographic locations, often interconnected via a network. Daemons in such environments are responsible for handling various tasks such as message passing, data synchronization, load balancing, fault tolerance, and ensuring that different components of the system work harmoniously. Understanding the role of daemons in distributed systems is essential for building and maintaining scalable, reliable, and efficient infrastructure.

In a distributed system, daemons often serve as the backbone that ensures smooth communication between nodes and the coordination of tasks. These processes run in the background, invisible to users, and often function without direct interaction. Each daemon in a distributed system may be responsible for a specific function, such as managing network connections, monitoring system health, or coordinating distributed file systems. For instance, in a distributed database system, a daemon may be responsible for handling replication and ensuring that data is synchronized across multiple nodes in real time. In a web server farm, multiple daemons may be responsible for load balancing incoming traffic across different servers to ensure that no single server becomes overwhelmed.

A key challenge in distributed systems is ensuring that all nodes remain consistent and synchronized despite being geographically dispersed or operating under different conditions. Daemons help manage this consistency by handling communication protocols between nodes and ensuring that data is propagated correctly. For example, in a distributed file system, daemons ensure that data updates made on one node are replicated to all other nodes in the system, maintaining consistency across the entire network. These daemons must be designed to handle network partitions, where nodes temporarily lose the ability to communicate with each other. In such cases, the daemons must ensure that any updates are eventually propagated once the network connection is restored, maintaining the integrity of the data.

Another important function of daemons in distributed systems is fault tolerance. Since distributed systems are composed of multiple independent components, failures are inevitable. Hardware failures, network issues, or software bugs can cause individual nodes to become unavailable, which can impact the overall performance of the system. Daemons help mitigate the impact of such failures by monitoring the health of the system and automatically recovering from failures when possible. For example, a distributed system might employ a daemon responsible for detecting failed nodes and automatically redistributing tasks to healthy nodes. In cloud computing environments, daemons ensure that services continue running even when a specific instance goes down, by provisioning new instances or rerouting traffic to healthy ones.

In addition to managing fault tolerance, daemons are also critical for load balancing in distributed systems. As the workload is distributed across multiple nodes, daemons help ensure that tasks are assigned to the appropriate nodes based on their available resources, such as CPU power, memory, or network bandwidth. Load balancing daemons continuously monitor the performance of different nodes and adjust the distribution of tasks to prevent overloading any single node. This dynamic load balancing is especially crucial in systems that experience fluctuating traffic, such as web servers or cloud-based applications, where demand can vary significantly over time.

In a distributed system, communication between nodes is another essential function that is handled by daemons. These daemons are responsible for ensuring that messages are sent, received, and processed across the network. They handle the complexities of network communication, including establishing connections, managing session states, and ensuring that messages are delivered reliably. For instance, in a messaging queue system, a daemon may be responsible for receiving and dispatching messages to the appropriate nodes, ensuring that messages are processed in the correct order and that no messages are lost. In peer-to-peer distributed systems, daemons manage the discovery of peers, ensuring that nodes can communicate directly with each other without requiring a central server.

Security is another important consideration in distributed systems, and daemons play a critical role in enforcing security policies. In distributed environments, data is often transmitted over untrusted networks, making it vulnerable to interception or tampering. Daemons help secure communication between nodes by implementing encryption protocols, such as SSL/TLS, and by authenticating nodes to ensure that only trusted entities can participate in the system. Additionally, security daemons monitor the system for any unauthorized access attempts, logging any suspicious activity and alerting administrators to potential breaches. In large distributed systems, security daemons can help prevent attacks such as man-in-the-middle attacks, denial of service (DoS) attacks, and unauthorized data access.

One of the challenges with daemons in distributed systems is ensuring scalability. As distributed systems grow, the number of nodes and the complexity of managing these nodes increases. Daemons must be designed to scale efficiently as the system expands, ensuring that they can handle larger volumes of data, more complex communication patterns, and higher numbers of nodes. This scalability involves optimizing daemons for performance, minimizing resource usage, and ensuring that they can operate efficiently even under heavy load. For example, a daemon in a distributed database system might need to handle an increasing number of queries as the database grows, while maintaining low latency and high throughput.

Daemons in distributed systems must also be fault-tolerant, ensuring that the system continues to function correctly even in the face of individual node failures. This often involves replicating data across multiple nodes and using consensus algorithms to ensure that updates to the system are consistent, even when some nodes are temporarily unavailable. In systems that require high availability, daemons are responsible for detecting failures and automatically rerouting traffic to healthy nodes or initiating failover procedures. This helps ensure that the system remains available and responsive to users, even when components fail.

Finally, the management and monitoring of daemons in distributed systems are crucial for maintaining system health and performance. Daemons that manage distributed resources need to be continuously monitored to ensure they are operating as expected. Monitoring daemons track the health of services, providing real-time information about their performance, resource utilization, and status. Alerts can be configured to notify administrators when services go down, experience performance degradation, or encounter errors. Daemon management tools allow administrators to start, stop, restart, or reconfigure daemons as needed, ensuring that the system continues to operate smoothly.

Daemons in distributed systems are responsible for enabling communication, coordinating tasks, managing failures, and ensuring the system runs efficiently and securely. They perform a variety of critical roles, from load balancing and fault tolerance to managing resources and securing communications. As distributed systems grow and evolve, the complexity of managing these daemons also increases. However, with careful design and proper monitoring, daemons can help ensure that distributed systems remain robust, scalable, and secure, providing the foundation for reliable and high-performance infrastructure. The role of daemons in distributed systems is indispensable, and understanding their operation is crucial for building and maintaining such systems effectively.

Managing Background Processes with Daemons

In modern operating systems, background processes play a crucial role in ensuring that essential services are available without requiring direct user interaction. These processes, often referred to as daemons, run silently in the background, managing system operations such as networking, logging, file handling, and scheduled tasks. Daemons provide the necessary infrastructure that allows systems to function continuously, even when no users are actively interacting with the machine. Managing these background processes effectively is essential for system administrators, as it ensures that resources are utilized efficiently, that services are maintained, and that the system operates securely and reliably. This chapter delves into the management of background processes with daemons, focusing on how to handle these processes, ensure they operate correctly, and maintain system health.

At its core, a daemon is a program that runs in the background, typically without any direct user interface. Daemons are typically designed to start automatically at system boot, often by the system's init system, such as systemd on modern Linux systems. Once started, these processes remain active, waiting to handle specific tasks or respond to events. For example, web servers, database management systems, and email servers are all examples of daemons that run in the background, handling requests and processing data continuously. Since daemons are typically long-running processes, their management involves not only starting and stopping them but also ensuring that they function as intended over time.

A fundamental part of managing background processes with daemons is ensuring that they are correctly configured to start automatically during system boot. In Linux systems, this is usually achieved by configuring service unit files within systemd. These unit files contain information about the service, including how it should be started, stopped, restarted, and any dependencies it has on other services. For example, a service that manages web traffic might depend on a database service being available, and the unit file ensures that the web server starts only after the database is up and running. By configuring daemons to start automatically on boot, system administrators ensure that critical services are available as soon as the system is ready, reducing downtime and manual intervention.

Once a daemon is running, administrators must monitor it to ensure that it continues to operate as expected. Monitoring background processes is essential for identifying potential issues before they cause system failures or slowdowns. For example, a web server daemon might start experiencing high resource usage due to an increase in incoming traffic, and without proper monitoring, this could lead to server crashes or slow performance. Tools such as systemd's journalctl or other system monitoring tools, like htop and top, allow administrators to view the resource usage of running daemons. By keeping an eye on CPU, memory, and disk usage, administrators can ensure that background processes do not consume excessive resources, which could impact other critical services.

Additionally, administrators should configure logging for background processes to capture any issues or irregularities that may occur during the daemon's operation. Logs provide valuable insights into the behavior of daemons, especially when diagnosing issues or understanding why a particular process failed or encountered errors. Most daemons use the system logging mechanism, such as syslog or systemd's built-in journaling system, to write logs. These logs can be used to track everything from routine operations to critical errors that require attention. Ensuring that logs are properly managed, rotated, and stored allows administrators to maintain historical data, which can be useful for debugging, troubleshooting, and ensuring that no critical information is lost.

Another important aspect of managing background processes is ensuring that daemons are secure. Since daemons often run with elevated privileges, such as root or administrative access, they can be a potential security risk if compromised. Limiting the privileges of daemons is crucial for reducing the attack surface. One common method is to configure daemons to run under a non-privileged user account. This principle of least privilege ensures that even if a daemon is exploited, the potential damage is limited because the attacker does not gain full control of the system. Additionally, secure communication protocols, such as SSL/TLS, should be used to protect data transmitted between daemons, especially when dealing with sensitive information. Daemons should also be configured to handle authentication and authorization, ensuring that only trusted entities can communicate with them.

When managing daemons, administrators must also be able to respond to failures. Daemons can encounter issues that cause them to stop running, either due to crashes, configuration errors, or resource exhaustion. To address this, systemd and other service management systems provide mechanisms for restarting daemons automatically when they fail. By configuring the Restart directive in the unit file, administrators can ensure that a daemon is restarted automatically if it crashes or becomes unresponsive. In some cases, administrators may need to limit the number of restart attempts to avoid creating an endless loop of failed processes. Properly managing daemon restarts helps maintain system stability by ensuring that services remain available without manual intervention.

In distributed systems or systems that rely on multiple daemons working together, managing the communication between these background processes is equally important. Daemons often need to communicate with each other to share data or coordinate tasks. For example, in a distributed database system, a daemon might need to synchronize data between multiple nodes. Effective inter-daemon communication requires careful planning to ensure that data is transmitted securely and efficiently. Tools like message queues, remote procedure calls (RPC), and inter-process communication (IPC) mechanisms are commonly used to facilitate communication between daemons. Ensuring that these communication mechanisms are properly configured and monitored is essential for the proper functioning of distributed systems.

Resource management is another critical aspect of managing background processes. Daemons consume system resources, such as CPU, memory, and disk space, and it is essential to ensure that they are efficiently using those resources. When configuring a daemon, administrators should set appropriate limits on the resources the daemon can consume, preventing any single process from consuming all available resources. In cases where multiple daemons are competing for resources, it may be necessary to prioritize certain daemons over others to ensure that the most critical services have access to the resources they need. Tools like nice and cgroups can be used to control resource allocation and prevent background processes from overwhelming the system.

Finally, regular maintenance is necessary to ensure that daemons continue to function as expected over time. Over time, daemon configurations may need to be updated, new features may be added, or the system environment may change. Regular updates, such as installing security patches and making performance optimizations, are essential for keeping background processes running smoothly. Administrators should also periodically review the configuration of running daemons to ensure that they align with evolving system requirements and that they continue to operate in a secure and efficient manner.

Managing background processes with daemons is a key aspect of system administration. By configuring daemons to start automatically, monitoring their performance, ensuring security, and addressing failures, administrators can ensure that their systems remain reliable and efficient. Properly managed daemons help maintain system stability, reduce downtime, and improve performance, allowing organizations to provide continuous services to users and applications. Understanding how to manage and maintain daemons is essential for anyone responsible for maintaining the health and performance of UNIX-like systems.

Using Daemons for Automation and Monitoring

In the world of system administration, automation and monitoring are critical aspects of maintaining an efficient, reliable, and secure system. Daemons, those background processes running on a UNIX-like system, are often the cornerstone for implementing these tasks. By leveraging daemons, administrators can automate repetitive system tasks, monitor the health and performance of critical services, and even detect and respond to potential issues before they become severe problems. Understanding how to utilize daemons for automation and monitoring is an essential skill for anyone managing a complex system or network. These daemons can be configured to perform specific functions, run in the background continuously, and take actions based on predefined conditions, enabling systems to operate with minimal human intervention.

One of the most fundamental uses of daemons for automation is in performing scheduled tasks. Daemons like cron and systemd timers are designed to automate processes by running specific commands or scripts at scheduled intervals. The cron daemon is one of the oldest and most widely used daemons in UNIX-like systems. It allows administrators to set up recurring tasks, such as system backups, log rotations, and software updates, without manual intervention. A cron job is typically set up by editing a configuration file that specifies when the task should run (for example, every day at midnight or every Monday morning) and which command or script to execute. This enables administrators to schedule complex tasks like data backups or clearing cache files at times when the system is under minimal load, ensuring optimal performance while maintaining the system's functionality.

Systemd, the modern init system used by many Linux distributions, offers more advanced automation capabilities through systemd timers. These timers allow for a wide range of scheduling and automation tasks, providing greater flexibility than cron. For example, systemd timers can trigger actions based on specific events or system states, such as when a service starts, when the system reboots, or when a particular log message is generated. Systemd timers are defined through unit files, where administrators can specify the time intervals or conditions under which the daemon should be triggered. This makes systemd an ideal tool for automating complex workflows or orchestrating services across multiple machines in a networked environment. Through these mechanisms, daemons enable administrators to automate tasks such as software installation, resource management, and service monitoring with a high degree of precision.

In addition to automation, daemons play a critical role in system monitoring. Monitoring is essential for understanding the health of a system, detecting performance bottlenecks, and identifying potential issues before they escalate into serious problems. Daemons used for monitoring run continuously in the background, gathering data on system performance, resource usage, and service health. These monitoring daemons can track key metrics such as CPU load, memory usage, disk space, network traffic, and the status of running services, providing administrators with real-time insights into system activity.

One common use of daemons for monitoring is to track system logs. Daemons like syslog and the systemd journal collect logs from various system processes, applications, and services. These logs provide a detailed record of events, errors, and warnings that can help administrators detect and troubleshoot issues. For instance, if a daemon encounters an error while handling a request, it can log the error and alert the administrator to the issue. Log-based monitoring allows administrators to identify patterns in system behavior, such as repeated failures or resource exhaustion, which can indicate potential problems that require attention.

Daemons can also be used to monitor the health of individual services and take corrective actions when necessary. For example, a daemon that monitors the web server might be configured to check the server's availability periodically. If the server becomes unresponsive or encounters an error, the monitoring daemon can automatically restart the service, preventing downtime. Some advanced monitoring daemons integrate with alerting systems, sending notifications via email, SMS, or messaging platforms like Slack whenever a service goes down or encounters an issue. This ensures that administrators are promptly informed and can take action before the issue affects users or applications.

Moreover, monitoring daemons can be configured to track system resources and ensure they are being used efficiently. For example, a daemon might monitor CPU usage and send an alert if it exceeds a predefined threshold, indicating that a process is consuming too much CPU time and could be throttling the system's performance. Similarly, daemons can monitor memory usage to detect memory leaks, disk space to identify storage issues, or network bandwidth to prevent congestion. These daemons often work in conjunction with other automation tools to trigger responses or escalate issues based on the severity of the monitoring data.

For large-scale systems or distributed environments, daemons can be used to monitor not just individual machines but entire networks or clusters. Monitoring daemons in such environments are often part of more extensive distributed monitoring systems, such as Prometheus, Nagios, or Zabbix, which collect and aggregate data from multiple sources and present it on centralized dashboards. These systems provide an overview of the health of the entire infrastructure, enabling administrators to identify potential failures across many machines and services. Distributed monitoring daemons are especially useful for cloud environments or large enterprise networks where keeping track of multiple services and systems manually would be impractical.

Automation and monitoring with daemons can also be integrated with other parts of the system to create more sophisticated management workflows. For instance, an automation daemon that manages system updates can be combined with a monitoring daemon that checks the health of system components. If the monitoring daemon detects a problem after an update is applied, it can trigger a series of corrective actions, such as rolling back the update or restarting the affected services. Similarly, if a daemon detects that a system is running low on resources, it might trigger an automated process to clean up temporary files, optimize databases, or balance workloads across multiple nodes in a distributed system.

Daemons that handle automation and monitoring are typically lightweight, designed to consume minimal resources while running in the background. However, it is crucial to configure them efficiently to avoid overloading the system with unnecessary processes. This can involve setting appropriate limits on memory usage, adjusting the frequency of monitoring checks, and ensuring that automation tasks are scheduled during off-peak hours. Proper configuration ensures that daemons do not interfere with system performance, allowing them to run smoothly without introducing unnecessary overhead.

The role of daemons in automation and monitoring is indispensable for modern system administration. By automating routine tasks, ensuring that services remain available, and proactively detecting potential issues, daemons help administrators maintain a high level of system reliability, performance, and security. Their continuous operation in the background ensures that systems function smoothly, minimizing downtime and optimizing resource utilization. Whether automating tasks such as backups and updates or providing real-time monitoring of services and system resources, daemons form the backbone of efficient system management in both small-scale and large-scale environments.

Advanced Daemon Configuration

Daemons are the backbone of many operating systems, silently running in the background to provide vital services, perform routine tasks, and ensure system stability. While basic daemon configuration may suffice for simple use cases, more advanced configurations are often required for managing complex systems, ensuring optimal performance, scalability, and security. These advanced configurations are essential for fine-tuning daemon behavior, optimizing resource utilization, and integrating daemons into larger system management frameworks. This chapter explores advanced daemon configuration, covering topics such as resource management, failure recovery, inter-service communication, and security considerations.

At the heart of advanced daemon configuration lies an understanding of how daemons interact with system resources. Daemons often run for extended periods, consuming system resources such as memory, CPU, and disk I/O. For performance reasons, it is crucial to configure daemons to ensure they are efficient and do not cause excessive resource consumption. One way to optimize daemon performance is by setting resource limits. For example, administrators can configure daemons to run with specific CPU or memory limits, ensuring that they do not monopolize system resources. These limits can be set using various mechanisms, such as the systemd unit files, which allow administrators to specify resource constraints for each daemon, ensuring they do not negatively impact the overall system.

In addition to setting resource limits, administrators can fine-tune the scheduling priorities of daemons. By adjusting the priority of a daemon process, system administrators can ensure that critical services receive the necessary CPU time while less critical background tasks are deprioritized. This can be particularly important in systems with high workloads, where balancing CPU usage across multiple daemons is necessary for maintaining overall system responsiveness. The nice and renice commands can be used to adjust the priority of running daemons, allowing administrators to control how resources are allocated based on the importance of the task at hand.

Failure recovery and fault tolerance are also key components of advanced daemon configuration. In complex systems, daemons must be able to recover gracefully from failures, ensuring minimal disruption to services. This often involves configuring daemons to automatically restart upon failure, a feature that can be implemented through system management tools such as systemd. By specifying restart directives within a systemd unit file, administrators can configure daemons to restart automatically if they crash or fail to respond to service requests. For example, the Restart=on-failure directive ensures that the daemon is automatically restarted if it exits with a non-zero exit status. This can be critical for ensuring the availability of services, particularly in production environments where downtime can result in significant operational losses.

Furthermore, administrators may configure daemons to handle specific failure scenarios more intelligently. Some daemons may need to perform cleanup operations or take corrective actions before restarting, such as saving state information, closing open file handles, or releasing resources. By configuring the daemon to use custom failure recovery scripts, administrators can ensure that the daemon shuts down cleanly and restarts without introducing issues that could impact system stability. This level of granularity allows for more precise control over how daemons handle failures, improving the overall reliability of the system.

Inter-service communication is another crucial aspect of advanced daemon configuration. In many modern systems, multiple daemons are responsible for different services, and these services often need to communicate with each other to perform tasks. For example, a web server daemon may need to communicate with a database daemon to retrieve data for users. Configuring daemons to communicate efficiently and securely is essential for maintaining a smooth workflow between services. This often involves setting up inter-process communication (IPC) mechanisms, such as message queues, shared memory, or sockets.

Sockets are one of the most commonly used IPC mechanisms for daemon communication. A daemon can listen on a specific socket for incoming requests from other processes or services. By configuring socket-based communication, daemons can receive and respond to messages or data requests in real time, without requiring direct user interaction. Additionally, administrators can configure socket activation with tools like systemd, which allows daemons to be started automatically when a connection is made to the socket. This can improve system efficiency by only starting services when needed, conserving system resources during idle periods.

In distributed systems, daemons often need to communicate across multiple nodes. This can be more complex, as the daemons must be configured to handle network communication securely and reliably. Daemons in such systems must be configured with proper network settings, including IP addresses, port numbers, and communication protocols, to ensure that they can connect with other daemons across the network. To avoid potential security vulnerabilities, communication between distributed daemons should always be encrypted using secure protocols such as SSL/TLS. By securing inter-daemon communication, administrators can prevent unauthorized access and ensure the integrity of the data being exchanged.

Security considerations play a significant role in advanced daemon configuration. Daemons often operate with elevated privileges, which makes them a prime target for attackers. Proper security measures are essential to protect daemons from being exploited. One of the most important aspects of securing a daemon is ensuring that it runs with the least privilege necessary for its operation. This is typically done by configuring the daemon to run as a non-privileged user, restricting its access to sensitive system resources. In systemd, this can be accomplished by specifying the User and Group directives in the unit file, ensuring that the daemon does not have access to resources that are not needed for its function.

Additionally, security daemons, such as intrusion detection systems (IDS), should be configured to monitor for any unusual activity, ensuring that potential security breaches are detected early. These daemons can be configured to check for specific patterns of activity, such as excessive failed login attempts, unusual network traffic, or attempts to exploit known vulnerabilities. By leveraging these monitoring daemons, administrators can take proactive steps to secure the system and mitigate potential threats.

Daemon configurations should also include mechanisms for logging and auditing. Daemons generate a significant amount of log data, which can be invaluable for troubleshooting and security monitoring. It is essential to ensure that logs are written to secure locations, with appropriate access controls in place to prevent unauthorized tampering. In addition to configuring the logging level, administrators should also configure log rotation to ensure that logs do not consume excessive disk space. Tools like logrotate can be used to manage log file sizes, ensuring that they remain manageable while retaining critical historical data.

Finally, managing daemon configurations requires careful documentation. As systems grow in complexity, it becomes more difficult to track the configuration of each daemon, particularly when dealing with a large number of daemons running across multiple servers. Maintaining detailed documentation of each daemon's configuration, dependencies, and performance characteristics is essential for ensuring that the system remains maintainable over time.

This documentation should be regularly updated to reflect any changes made to the daemon's configuration or the overall system architecture.

Advanced daemon configuration is essential for optimizing performance, ensuring reliability, and maintaining security in complex systems. By carefully configuring resource usage, automating failure recovery, enabling inter-service communication, and addressing security concerns, administrators can ensure that daemons run efficiently and securely. These configurations play a critical role in the stability and efficiency of a system, helping to automate routine tasks, ensure services are available, and protect against security threats. Whether running a single server or managing a large distributed system, mastering advanced daemon configuration is vital for ensuring that systems remain responsive and secure.

Configuring Daemon Resource Limits

In any operating system, efficient resource management is essential to ensuring optimal performance and maintaining system stability. Daemons, which are background processes running without direct user interaction, play a critical role in the functioning of these systems. They handle a variety of tasks, such as managing network services, performing system maintenance, and handling requests from users or other processes. However, because daemons often run for extended periods, they can consume significant system resources, including CPU, memory, and disk space. Without proper resource management, daemons can monopolize system resources, leading to degraded performance or even system instability. Configuring daemon resource limits is a vital aspect of system administration that helps ensure that daemons do not overwhelm the system or interfere with other critical processes.

Resource limits for daemons serve to control the amount of system resources that each daemon can consume. These limits are essential for maintaining a balance between the various processes running on the system. When configuring resource limits for daemons, administrators are essentially defining constraints on how much CPU time, memory, and other resources the daemon can use. By doing so, administrators can prevent a single daemon from consuming excessive resources, which could lead to slowdowns, crashes, or other adverse effects on the system's performance.

One of the most common types of resource limits for daemons is CPU usage. CPU time is a critical resource on any system, and daemons that consume too much CPU time can slow down other processes, including critical services. The operating system provides various ways to control CPU usage by daemons, including the ability to limit the priority at which a daemon runs. In Linux-based systems, tools like nice and renice can be used to adjust the priority of a daemon process. By lowering the priority of a daemon, administrators can ensure that more important tasks are given higher priority for CPU time. For example, a web server daemon may be configured to run with a lower priority than a database daemon to ensure that database queries are processed with the highest priority.

Another method of controlling CPU usage is by setting limits on the amount of time a daemon is allowed to use the CPU. In Linux systems, this can be done by configuring the ulimit command, which allows administrators to set limits on the number of processes, file descriptors, and other resources that a user or process can consume. For daemons, resource limits can be set in the service's configuration file or systemd unit file, ensuring that the daemon cannot exceed a certain threshold of CPU usage. By setting these limits, administrators can prevent any single daemon from monopolizing the CPU, ensuring that other processes are not starved of resources.

Memory management is another critical aspect of daemon resource limits. Daemons that consume too much memory can lead to system slowdowns or, in extreme cases, cause the system to run out of memory entirely. This can result in system crashes, instability, or the operating system resorting to swapping memory to disk, which significantly reduces performance. To avoid these issues, administrators can configure memory limits for daemons, ensuring that they do not exceed a predefined amount of memory. In Linux systems, this can be done using cgroups (control groups), which allow administrators to allocate specific amounts of memory to different processes or daemons. By assigning memory limits through cgroups, administrators can prevent daemons from using excessive memory and ensure that the system remains responsive even under heavy load.

In addition to limiting CPU and memory usage, administrators may also need to configure limits on other system resources, such as file descriptors, network bandwidth, and disk space. File descriptors are used by processes to interact with files, sockets, and other system resources. If a daemon opens too many file descriptors, it can cause the system to run out of available file handles, which can lead to errors or crashes. To prevent this, administrators can set a limit on the number of file descriptors a daemon can open. In Linux, this can be done using the ulimit command or by configuring the daemon's service unit file in systemd to define the LimitNOFILE directive, which sets the maximum number of file descriptors the daemon can use.

Similarly, network bandwidth can also be a limiting factor for daemons, especially in systems that handle large volumes of network traffic. By setting limits on the amount of bandwidth a daemon can consume, administrators can ensure that no single service monopolizes the network, leaving other processes or services starved for bandwidth. This can be particularly important in multi-tenant environments, where different users or applications share the same network resources. Daemons that interact with the network, such as web servers, database servers, and proxy servers, can be configured to limit the amount of bandwidth they consume, ensuring fair resource allocation and preventing network congestion.

Disk space is another resource that must be managed when configuring daemons. Daemons that generate large amounts of log data or store temporary files can quickly consume available disk space, leading to potential issues such as system slowdowns or file system full errors. Administrators can configure log rotation for daemons to ensure that log files do not grow unchecked, consuming all available disk space. Log rotation can be set up using tools such as logrotate, which automatically rotates and compresses old log files, ensuring that disk space is efficiently used without sacrificing important historical data.

The configuration of resource limits for daemons is not only about preventing resource exhaustion but also about ensuring that daemons can run efficiently and reliably within the available system resources.

Resource limits must be carefully balanced to allow daemons to perform their tasks without overburdening the system. Setting limits that are too strict may result in daemons being unable to perform their functions adequately, while setting limits that are too generous can lead to system instability. Therefore, administrators must monitor system performance and adjust resource limits as necessary to maintain a balance between resource usage and performance.

Monitoring the resource usage of daemons is an essential part of managing their resource limits. By using monitoring tools like top, htop, or systemd's journalctl, administrators can track how much CPU, memory, and other resources a daemon is using in real time. This allows administrators to identify any daemons that may be consuming more resources than expected and make adjustments to their resource limits. For example, if a daemon is consuming an excessive amount of memory, the administrator may need to reduce its memory limit or optimize its code to reduce memory consumption. Monitoring provides valuable insights that help administrators make informed decisions about resource allocation.

Configuring daemon resource limits is an essential aspect of system administration, particularly in environments where system resources must be shared among many processes and services. By setting limits on CPU usage, memory, file descriptors, network bandwidth, and disk space, administrators can ensure that daemons run efficiently without causing system instability or performance degradation. Careful management of these resources, coupled with regular monitoring, ensures that daemons can perform their tasks without negatively impacting the overall system performance, creating a more stable and efficient environment for both users and services. Proper resource limits not only help maintain system health but also contribute to better scalability, security, and reliability.

Daemon Communication: IPC and Sockets

In any multi-process or distributed system, communication between processes is a critical component for ensuring that different services and components can interact efficiently. Daemons, which are background processes that perform tasks without direct user interaction, often need to communicate with other processes, whether they are local to the same system or distributed across a network. For this communication to be effective, daemons rely on various methods of inter-process communication (IPC), with two of the most commonly used methods being sockets and other IPC mechanisms. Understanding how daemons communicate, the role of IPC, and the types of sockets they use is fundamental for system administrators and developers working with complex systems and services.

IPC is a set of mechanisms that allow processes to communicate with each other. This is particularly important in systems where multiple processes need to share data or coordinate actions. Since daemons typically run in the background, they often need to exchange information with other daemons, applications, or services. IPC allows these processes to send and receive messages, share data, or synchronize actions in a way that is efficient, reliable, and secure. For instance, a web server daemon might need to communicate with a database daemon to retrieve data requested by users, or a monitoring daemon may need to communicate with other system processes to check their status and health.

Sockets, as one of the most important IPC mechanisms, provide a versatile way for processes to communicate, both locally and over a network. A socket is essentially an endpoint for sending or receiving data across a network, allowing processes to exchange information through well-defined protocols. In the context of daemons, sockets can be used for communication both between processes on the same machine and between processes on different machines connected via a network. Communication over sockets is usually done using the Transmission Control Protocol (TCP) or the User Datagram Protocol (UDP), both of which are integral to many networked services. For local communication on the same machine, UNIX domain sockets are often used, as they provide a fast, reliable method of IPC without involving the network stack.

The use of sockets for communication between daemons is crucial for systems that are designed to handle a large number of concurrent requests or operate in a distributed environment. For example, in a web application, the web server daemon (e.g., Apache or Nginx) often communicates with the application server daemon via TCP sockets. These daemons might be running on separate machines or containers within a cloud-based architecture. Through socket communication, they can exchange data, share state information, and handle user requests in real time. Similarly, a database daemon often communicates with the web server or application server via TCP sockets to process database queries.

UNIX domain sockets, on the other hand, are specifically designed for communication between processes on the same machine. They are more efficient than TCP/IP sockets for local communication because they bypass the network stack, leading to faster data transfer. UNIX domain sockets are commonly used in systems where processes need to interact on the same machine, such as when a daemon communicates with a local service or another local process. For example, the MySQL database daemon might use UNIX domain sockets to communicate with a local web server, ensuring low-latency access to the database.

In addition to sockets, daemons often rely on other IPC mechanisms to exchange information. These can include pipes, message queues, shared memory, and semaphores, which are all commonly used in UNIX-like systems for process coordination and data exchange. For instance, a daemon might use pipes to send the output of one process to another, or it might use message queues to send data between processes asynchronously. These IPC methods allow daemons to operate independently while still enabling them to communicate with each other, ensuring smooth and efficient system operation.

When configuring daemons for communication, it is important to consider security. Since daemons often run with elevated privileges, allowing them to interact with sensitive system resources, it is essential to ensure that their communication channels are secure and that only authorized processes can access them. This is particularly important for networked daemons, where data can potentially be intercepted or tampered with during transmission. To address these concerns, communication between daemons should be encrypted, especially when sensitive data is being exchanged. Protocols like SSL/TLS can be used to secure the data transmitted between daemons, ensuring confidentiality and integrity. For local communication, UNIX domain sockets can also be secured using file system permissions, limiting access to trusted users and processes.

Furthermore, ensuring that daemon communication does not interfere with other system processes is important for maintaining system stability and performance. Daemons must be designed to handle communication in an efficient manner, without consuming excessive resources or causing bottlenecks. For instance, daemons should be optimized for non-blocking I/O operations when using sockets or other IPC mechanisms to prevent one process from waiting indefinitely for another to respond. This is particularly important in high-performance systems, where delays in one part of the system can have cascading effects on other processes.

To ensure that daemons can efficiently handle communication under various conditions, they must be configured to manage timeouts and retries. For example, if a daemon is waiting for a response from another process and the communication takes too long, it should be able to handle this scenario gracefully, either by retrying the operation or by reporting an error without causing the entire system to stall. Timeouts can be configured for socket connections, ensuring that daemons do not hang indefinitely while waiting for data. Similarly, retry logic can be implemented to allow daemons to attempt communication with other services multiple times before giving up or taking corrective action.

In distributed systems, daemons often need to maintain consistent state information across multiple nodes, ensuring that data is synchronized and available even when some nodes are temporarily unavailable. This requires daemons to communicate efficiently over the network and handle situations where network partitions or node failures occur. Protocols like consensus algorithms (e.g., Paxos or Raft) can be used to coordinate communication between daemons in a distributed environment, ensuring that updates to shared data are consistent across all nodes. In this context, daemons must be able to handle communication failures, ensuring that they can recover and synchronize once the network is restored.

In some cases, daemons may also need to implement mechanisms for message persistence to ensure that communication is not lost in the event of a failure. For example, a messaging daemon may need to store messages temporarily in a queue until the recipient process is ready to consume them. This persistence ensures that critical information is not lost, even if the recipient daemon is temporarily down or unavailable.

The ability of daemons to communicate efficiently and securely through IPC and sockets is central to the operation of modern systems. From enabling local communication to supporting complex distributed architectures, daemons rely on these communication mechanisms to function effectively. By configuring daemons to use appropriate IPC methods, ensuring secure communication channels, and implementing robust error handling, system administrators can ensure that their services remain reliable, efficient, and secure. Effective communication between daemons is key to the overall health of the system, and understanding how to manage and optimize this communication is essential for maintaining a well-functioning and resilient infrastructure.

FS and Cron Integration for Automated Backups

Automated backups are an essential part of system administration, ensuring that critical data is consistently backed up without requiring manual intervention. A reliable backup strategy is vital for system recovery in case of failure, corruption, or other unforeseen circumstances. In the context of UNIX-like systems, two tools that play a crucial role in setting up automated backup processes are the File System (FS) and the Cron daemon. By integrating these tools, system administrators can create an efficient and reliable backup solution that runs periodically, ensuring that important data is never lost and that the system is protected against disasters.

The file system (FS) in UNIX-like operating systems is the primary way data is stored and organized. It defines how files are named, stored, and retrieved. It also handles file permissions, access control, and system integrity. Understanding the underlying file system structure is essential when setting up automated backups, as it allows administrators to target specific files, directories, or even entire systems for backup. The backup process typically involves copying files and directories to a secure location, such as a remote server, cloud storage, or an external drive, where they can be easily restored in the event of data loss.

In conjunction with the file system, the Cron daemon is a powerful tool for automating tasks at scheduled intervals. Cron allows system administrators to set up recurring jobs, such as running scripts or executing commands, at specific times or dates. It is an ideal tool for scheduling automated backups because it ensures that the backup process runs at the desired intervals without requiring constant human intervention. The integration of Cron with the file system enables administrators to create backups of important directories or entire file systems at regular intervals, ensuring that up-to-date copies of critical data are always available.

Setting up automated backups using Cron and the file system involves creating a backup script that specifies the files or directories to be backed up, the destination where the backups should be stored, and any additional options or parameters required for the backup process. The script typically uses tools such as tar, rsync, or cp to copy files to the backup location. For example, a simple script might use tar to create a compressed archive of a directory and then transfer that archive to a remote server using scp or rsync. The backup script can be configured to run at specific intervals using Cron, ensuring that backups are performed regularly without manual oversight.

To configure automated backups, administrators first need to create a Cron job that defines when the backup script will run. Cron jobs are defined in the crontab file, which specifies the time and frequency of the job. The crontab file consists of a series of time fields that define the minute, hour, day of the month, month, and day of the week when a specific command should be executed. For example, to create a backup job that runs every day at 2:00 AM, an administrator would add the following line to the crontab file:

0 2 * * * /path/to/backup_script.sh

This line tells Cron to run the backup script located at /path/to/backup_script.sh at 2:00 AM every day. By using Cron, administrators can set up daily, weekly, or monthly backups based on their needs. Additionally, Cron allows for flexible scheduling, such as running backups only on specific weekdays or during certain hours, enabling administrators to schedule backups during off-peak times to minimize the impact on system performance.

When integrating Cron with the file system for automated backups, it is important to consider the nature of the data being backed up and the appropriate backup strategy. There are several approaches to backing up data, including full backups, incremental backups, and differential backups. A full backup involves copying all the files in a specified directory or file system, while an incremental backup only copies files that have changed since the last backup. A differential backup, on the other hand, copies all files that have changed since the last full backup. Each approach has its advantages and trade-offs in terms of storage space, speed, and recovery time.

For example, if an administrator wants to back up an entire file system regularly, they might choose to perform full backups once a week and incremental backups daily. This combination allows for a comprehensive backup strategy that ensures minimal data loss while minimizing the storage space required for the backups. By using rsync in the backup script, administrators can easily create incremental backups by specifying the --link-dest option, which tells rsync to only copy files that have been modified since the last backup.

Another important consideration when setting up automated backups is ensuring that the backups are stored in a secure and reliable location. The backup destination can be a local storage device, such as an external hard drive, or a remote server, such as a network-attached storage (NAS) device or a cloud storage service. The backup destination should be chosen based on the system's needs, the volume of data, and the desired level of redundancy. For example, storing backups on a remote server provides an added layer of protection against data loss in the event of a hardware failure on the local machine. In such cases, administrators may configure their backup script to use secure protocols like rsync or scp to transfer backup files to the remote destination.

Additionally, administrators should ensure that backup files are stored in a manner that allows for easy recovery. This may involve organizing backup files with meaningful filenames that include timestamps or using directory structures that mirror the original file system layout. By organizing backups in this way, administrators can quickly locate and restore specific files or directories in the event of data loss. It is also a good practice to test backup and restoration procedures regularly to verify that backups are functioning correctly and that the system can be restored to a functional state if necessary.

Another important aspect of configuring automated backups is ensuring that backup logs are generated and reviewed. Backup logs provide a record of each backup operation, including information about the success or failure of the process, any errors encountered, and the number of files backed up. These logs can be invaluable for troubleshooting backup issues and verifying that backups are being performed as scheduled. By configuring the backup script to generate logs and using Cron to schedule periodic log reviews, administrators can stay informed about the status of their backup operations and take corrective action if necessary.

Automating backups using Cron and the file system is a powerful and flexible approach to ensuring data protection and system resilience. By leveraging Cron to schedule regular backups and using the file system tools to copy data to secure storage locations, administrators can create a reliable backup system that requires minimal manual intervention. With careful configuration, monitoring, and periodic testing, automated backups can help prevent data loss and ensure that critical systems can be restored quickly in the event of a failure.

Using Sysctl for Enhanced Security in Daemons

In UNIX-like operating systems, security is a primary concern for system administrators, especially when it comes to the management and operation of daemons. Daemons, which are background processes that provide essential services like web hosting, networking, or database management, often run with elevated privileges, making them attractive targets for attackers. Therefore, ensuring that these daemons operate within secure environments is crucial for maintaining the integrity and reliability of the entire system. One of the most effective tools for securing daemons is sysctl, a utility that allows administrators to configure kernel parameters at runtime. Through sysctl, administrators can fine-tune system security settings to mitigate vulnerabilities in daemons and improve overall system security.

Sysctl operates by manipulating kernel parameters, many of which directly affect the security posture of the system. These parameters control various aspects of the operating system's behavior, including networking, memory management, process handling, and security policies. For daemons that often handle network communication or interact with sensitive data, configuring these sysctl parameters can significantly reduce the attack surface, prevent unauthorized access, and harden the system against potential exploits.

One of the most important sysctl parameters for securing daemons is related to the system's networking stack. Since daemons often listen for incoming connections, particularly over TCP/IP, securing these connections is essential to prevent unauthorized access. Sysctl provides parameters like net.ipv4.conf.all.rp_filter and net.ipv4.conf.default.rp_filter, which control reverse path filtering. Reverse path filtering helps prevent IP spoofing attacks by ensuring that the source address of incoming packets matches the expected routing path. Enabling reverse path filtering at the kernel level ensures that daemons cannot inadvertently accept malicious or forged packets, which could otherwise be used to exploit vulnerabilities in network services.

Another vital sysctl parameter related to network security is net.ipv4.tcp_syncookies. This parameter enables or disables SYN cookies, a technique used to protect against SYN flood attacks, a form of denial-of-service (DoS) attack that targets the TCP handshake process. By enabling SYN cookies, the system can maintain the integrity of connections during heavy traffic or attack scenarios, preventing daemons from being overwhelmed by malicious connection attempts. This is particularly important for daemons that handle network services, as SYN flood attacks can lead to resource exhaustion and service unavailability.

For daemons that handle sensitive data or user authentication, such as SSH daemons, another key sysctl setting to configure is kernel.randomize_va_space. This parameter controls Address Space Layout Randomization (ASLR), a security feature designed to make it more difficult for attackers to predict the location of system memory, including libraries and executable code. By enabling ASLR through sysctl, administrators can make it harder for attackers to exploit vulnerabilities in daemons through techniques like buffer overflows, which rely on knowing the location of specific code or data in memory. Ensuring that ASLR is enabled on the system provides an additional layer of defense for daemons against such attacks.

Daemons often operate with root privileges or other elevated permissions, giving them significant access to system resources. To minimize the risk of privilege escalation, sysctl allows administrators to configure various security parameters that limit the capabilities of these processes. For example, the fs.suid_dumpable parameter controls whether a core dump can be generated for set-user-ID (SUID) programs. SUID programs, when executed, run with the privileges of the file owner, often root. Allowing core dumps for these programs can expose sensitive data that could be exploited by attackers. By setting fs.suid_dumpable to 0, administrators can prevent core dumps from being generated, thus protecting the system from leaking potentially valuable information.

Additionally, sysctl provides a range of parameters to control process behavior that can further enhance daemon security. The kernel.randomize_kstack_offset parameter, for example, randomizes the stack location for kernel threads, making it more difficult for attackers to predict where to inject malicious code into the kernel space. This adds another layer of protection, particularly for daemons running with elevated privileges, as it mitigates the risks associated with stack-based exploits.

The net.ipv4.ip_forward and net.ipv6.conf.all.forwarding parameters are also important for securing daemons involved in network routing. By default, many systems do not need to forward IP packets between different network interfaces unless they are explicitly configured as routers. Disabling IP forwarding on systems that do not require it can reduce the risk of unauthorized access to internal network resources and prevent daemons from becoming involuntary participants in attacks like IP spoofing or man-in-the-middle (MITM) attacks. Setting these parameters to 0 ensures that only daemons explicitly authorized to forward traffic are allowed to do so, enhancing overall network security.

In addition to the security-focused sysctl parameters, administrators can also use sysctl to enforce system-wide security policies for daemons. For example, the kernel.pid_max parameter limits the maximum number of process identifiers (PIDs) that can be assigned to processes on the system. By lowering this value, administrators can reduce the likelihood of process table exhaustion, which could otherwise enable attackers to exhaust system resources or manipulate process management to exploit vulnerable daemons.

Another critical aspect of daemon security is monitoring and auditing. Sysctl allows administrators to configure logging and auditing parameters that can help track daemon activities, detect anomalies, and respond quickly to potential threats. For example, auditctl can be used in conjunction with sysctl to log access attempts, changes in system configuration, or other suspicious activities related to daemon processes. This provides a useful mechanism for administrators to monitor daemons in real-time and ensure that no unauthorized actions are being carried out on the system.

Finally, administrators must consider the overall security of the system when configuring sysctl parameters for daemons. While individual daemon security settings are important, they should be part of a broader security strategy that includes secure configuration practices, regular patching, access controls, and network segmentation. Sysctl parameters should be tailored to the specific needs of each daemon, ensuring that each one operates securely and efficiently. Regular audits of these settings, along with ongoing security assessments, are critical to maintaining a robust security posture for daemons and the system as a whole.

By leveraging sysctl to configure security settings, administrators can significantly reduce the attack surface of daemons and ensure that they are running in a secure environment. Sysctl provides an invaluable toolset for enhancing the security of UNIX-like systems, helping to protect daemons from exploitation, prevent unauthorized access, and ensure the overall integrity of the system. With careful configuration, sysctl allows administrators to create a hardened environment that mitigates common attack vectors and provides a foundation for maintaining secure and resilient systems.

Combining Cron and Daemons for System Maintenance

System maintenance is a critical aspect of managing any server or computer system, ensuring that the system remains healthy, secure, and efficient. One of the most effective ways to automate and streamline system maintenance is by combining the power of Cron and daemons. Cron, a time-based job scheduler, allows administrators to schedule tasks to run at specific intervals, while daemons, which are background processes, handle the execution of tasks that keep the system functioning smoothly. Together, Cron and daemons can automate complex maintenance operations, monitor system health, back up data, and ensure that everything continues to run optimally with minimal manual intervention.

Cron is a simple yet powerful utility that enables administrators to automate the execution of tasks on a recurring basis. Cron jobs are defined in the crontab file, which contains the schedule and the commands that should be executed. This makes Cron an ideal tool for automating regular maintenance tasks, such as running backups, cleaning up temporary files, rotating logs, or updating software packages. Cron allows administrators to define jobs that run at specific times, whether on an hourly, daily, weekly, or monthly basis, or even at precise times of day. This enables system maintenance to be handled automatically, reducing the likelihood of human error and ensuring that critical tasks are not overlooked.

Daemons, on the other hand, are processes that run in the background, often without any direct user interaction. They are typically designed to perform essential services continuously or at scheduled intervals. Common examples of daemons include web servers, database servers, email servers, and monitoring services. These background processes play a central role in maintaining the system's functionality, responding to requests, managing resources, and ensuring that services remain available. Daemons often need to run on a consistent basis and handle long-running tasks that may need to be scheduled or triggered by specific events.

By combining Cron with daemons, administrators can set up a comprehensive system maintenance strategy that is both efficient and reliable. For example, a system that relies on regular backups can use a daemon to handle the backup process, while Cron ensures that the backups occur at specified times, such as once a day or once a week. The backup daemon can be configured to perform incremental backups, checking which files have changed since the last backup, and then compressing and storing those files in a secure location. Cron can then be used to schedule this backup daemon to run at night, when system load is lower, ensuring minimal impact on performance during business hours.

Similarly, system administrators can use Cron to schedule a cleanup daemon that removes temporary files, old logs, or other unnecessary data that accumulate over time. Temporary files can take up valuable disk space, slowing down the system and causing storage issues. By configuring a cleanup daemon to run periodically and invoking it via Cron, administrators can automate the process of clearing out these files, freeing up disk space and improving system performance. Cron can be set up to trigger the cleanup daemon every day at midnight or every week on a designated day, ensuring that the cleanup process occurs automatically and on schedule.

Another important use case for combining Cron and daemons in system maintenance is managing system updates. Operating systems and applications often release updates that address security vulnerabilities, bug fixes, and performance improvements. Keeping the system up to date is a crucial part of maintaining its security and efficiency. Daemons can be used to automatically download and install these updates, while Cron schedules when the updates should be applied. This can be done during off-peak hours to minimize disruption to users. By automating the update process with Cron and a dedicated update daemon, administrators can ensure that critical security patches are applied without requiring constant manual intervention.

Log rotation is another area where Cron and daemons work together to ensure smooth system operation. Log files can quickly grow in size, consuming valuable disk space and potentially affecting system performance. Daemons, such as logrotate, are often used to manage the size and rotation of log files, ensuring that older logs are archived or deleted as necessary. Cron can be used to schedule log rotation tasks at regular intervals, such as daily or weekly, ensuring that log files are properly managed without manual oversight. This process helps maintain the health of the file system, ensuring that logs do not consume excessive disk space and that older logs are kept in a manageable format for future reference.

Cron and daemons can also work together to monitor system health and performance. Monitoring daemons are responsible for tracking key metrics, such as CPU usage, memory usage, disk space, and network traffic. These daemons can be configured to send alerts when a certain threshold is exceeded, such as when disk space is running low or when a service becomes unresponsive. Cron can be used to schedule periodic checks and reports generated by monitoring daemons. For example, administrators might configure a daemon to check the system's health every hour, and Cron can be set to run a script that collects and compiles the health data into a report, which is then emailed to the system administrator. This ensures that administrators are notified of potential issues before they escalate into major problems, allowing for timely intervention.

System administrators can also use Cron and daemons to enforce security policies. Security daemons can be set up to monitor for suspicious activity, such as failed login attempts, unauthorized access to certain files, or unexpected changes to system configuration. Cron can schedule periodic security scans to run at designated times, such as weekly or monthly, to ensure that no unauthorized activity has occurred. Additionally, Cron can be used to schedule the automatic execution of security-related tasks, such as running vulnerability scans, updating antivirus definitions, or applying security patches. This approach ensures that security is always up to date and that potential threats are detected early, minimizing the risk of a breach.

Cron and daemons also enable system administrators to automate complex workflows and orchestration tasks. For example, in a multi-tier application environment, Cron can be used to schedule tasks that involve communication between different daemons. A backup daemon might need to trigger a service stop, perform the backup, and then restart the service once the backup is complete. This process can be fully automated using a combination of Cron, daemons, and custom scripts. This integration simplifies the management of complex systems and ensures that critical maintenance tasks are completed efficiently and consistently.

Combining Cron with daemons for system maintenance streamlines and automates the management of various system functions. Whether for backing up data, cleaning up disk space, applying updates, rotating logs, or monitoring system health, this integration reduces the need for manual intervention and ensures that maintenance tasks are completed consistently and on time. By using Cron and daemons in concert, administrators can ensure that the system remains stable, secure, and efficient without constant oversight, allowing them to focus on higher-level tasks and strategic initiatives. The power of Cron and daemons lies in their ability to work together to provide a seamless, automated approach to system maintenance.

Managing System Resources with Sysctl, NFS, and Cron

Efficient management of system resources is essential for maintaining optimal performance, security, and stability in any UNIX-like operating system. Various tools and utilities are available to system administrators to manage these resources effectively, including Sysctl, Network File System (NFS), and Cron. Each of these tools serves a unique purpose but can be integrated to manage different aspects of system resources, from kernel parameters to file system management and scheduled tasks. By leveraging Sysctl, NFS, and Cron together, administrators can create a cohesive and efficient resource management strategy that addresses a wide range of system needs.

Sysctl is a powerful utility that allows administrators to configure kernel parameters at runtime. These parameters control how the operating system behaves in various contexts, including network settings, memory management, and process handling. By adjusting these parameters, administrators can optimize system performance, enhance security, and prevent certain types of system failures. For example, the vm.swappiness parameter controls the kernel's tendency to swap memory pages to disk. By tuning this parameter, administrators can manage the system's memory usage more efficiently, ensuring that critical processes remain in memory while minimizing disk swapping. Another important parameter is fs.file-max, which defines the maximum number of file handles that the system can allocate. By configuring this parameter, administrators can prevent resource exhaustion, particularly on systems that handle a large number of open files.

One of the primary use cases for Sysctl in resource management is network performance tuning. Parameters such as net.ipv4.tcp_rmem and net.ipv4.tcp_wmem allow administrators to adjust the minimum, default, and maximum sizes of the receive and send buffers used by TCP connections. Tuning these settings can improve network performance, particularly in environments with high traffic volumes. Similarly, the net.ipv4.conf.all.arp_filter parameter can be configured to control how the system handles ARP requests, reducing the risk of network-based attacks and improving the efficiency of network communication. By fine-tuning these and other Sysctl parameters, administrators can ensure that the system is optimized for their specific workload, whether it involves heavy network traffic or memory-intensive applications.

In addition to Sysctl, the Network File System (NFS) plays a crucial role in resource management by providing a way to share files and directories across a network. NFS allows multiple systems to access and modify files as if they were local, simplifying the management of data in distributed environments. By mounting remote NFS shares, administrators can centralize data storage, distribute resources efficiently, and ensure that users on different systems have access to the same files. NFS can be particularly useful in managing resources across clusters of servers or in environments where multiple users need to access large datasets stored on a central server.

However, managing NFS comes with its own set of challenges. One of the primary concerns when using NFS is ensuring that file access is efficient and secure. To optimize NFS performance, administrators need to configure the NFS server and client settings properly. For example, the rsize and wsize parameters determine the maximum amount of data that can be read or written in a single NFS operation. Increasing these values can improve performance in high-bandwidth environments, but it may also lead to higher memory consumption. Administrators should balance these settings based on their network conditions and hardware capabilities.

Security is another important consideration when using NFS. NFS relies on the underlying network for file sharing, and improper configuration can expose sensitive data to unauthorized access. To mitigate this risk, administrators should ensure that NFS shares are properly secured. This can be achieved by using access control lists (ACLs) to restrict which users or hosts can access certain files or directories. Additionally, using NFS over secure connections, such as through VPNs or by implementing Kerberos authentication, can further enhance security by encrypting the data being transmitted.

NFS also provides administrators with the flexibility to configure automounting, which allows file systems to be mounted automatically when accessed. This is particularly useful in environments where remote file systems are used infrequently but need to be accessible when required. By configuring automounting, administrators can reduce the administrative overhead of manually mounting NFS shares, while ensuring that resources are available on demand.

While Sysctl and NFS are invaluable tools for managing system resources, Cron is equally important for automating routine tasks that are essential for maintaining system performance. Cron is a time-based job scheduler that allows administrators to automate tasks such as backups, log rotations, system updates, and performance monitoring. By using Cron, administrators can schedule these tasks to run at specific times or intervals, reducing the need for manual intervention and ensuring that system maintenance is performed consistently and reliably.

For example, administrators can use Cron to schedule backups of critical data stored on local or remote file systems. By running a backup script through Cron, administrators can ensure that data is regularly backed up without having to remember to initiate the process manually. Similarly, Cron can be used to automate log rotation tasks, ensuring that log files do not grow too large and consume excessive disk space. This is particularly important in systems that generate large amounts of log data, as unrotated logs can fill up the disk and cause performance issues or prevent the system from functioning properly.

Cron can also be used to automate performance monitoring tasks. By scheduling scripts that check system resource usage, administrators can track metrics such as CPU load, memory usage, and disk space over time. These metrics can then be logged and analyzed to identify trends or potential performance bottlenecks. In addition, Cron can be configured to run maintenance tasks, such as clearing temporary files, cleaning up caches, or restarting services that have become unresponsive. By automating these tasks, administrators can ensure that the system remains in optimal condition without requiring constant oversight.

The integration of Sysctl, NFS, and Cron creates a powerful framework for managing system resources. Sysctl allows for fine-grained control over kernel parameters that directly affect system performance, while NFS provides a flexible and efficient way to manage remote file access. Cron complements these tools by automating routine maintenance tasks, reducing the administrative burden on system administrators and ensuring that system resources are managed efficiently. Together, these tools can help administrators maintain system performance, security, and stability, ensuring that the system continues to run smoothly even as it scales to handle increased workloads.

By combining Sysctl, NFS, and Cron, administrators can implement a comprehensive strategy for managing system resources that addresses both performance and security needs. Through proper configuration and automation, administrators can create a system that is efficient, secure, and capable of handling the demands of a modern, distributed environment. Whether managing a small server or a large-scale infrastructure, the integration of these tools provides a robust foundation for ensuring that system resources are allocated effectively and that the system remains responsive and reliable over time.

Troubleshooting Daemons, NFS, and Cron Interactions

Troubleshooting is an essential skill for any system administrator, especially when dealing with complex interactions between different system components. Daemons, the background processes that provide essential services, often interact with each other and rely on resources provided by the system, such as the network file system (NFS) or scheduled tasks managed by Cron. When these components experience issues or fail to work as expected, it can be difficult to pinpoint the root cause. This chapter focuses on troubleshooting the interactions between daemons, NFS, and Cron, offering strategies for identifying and resolving common problems that may arise in a typical system environment.

Daemons are crucial for system operations, often running continuously and providing services like web hosting, database management, or email processing. When troubleshooting daemons, the first step is to understand the nature of their operation. Daemons generally run in the background, without direct user interaction, and are usually designed to restart automatically if they fail. However, when a daemon fails or behaves erratically, identifying the issue requires checking its status, logs, and configurations. The systemctl command, used to manage systemd-based services, is an essential tool for monitoring the status of daemons. Running systemctl status <daemon_name> provides real-time information about the daemon's health, including its active state, error messages, and recent activity. If a daemon fails to start or crashes unexpectedly, the logs generated by the daemon can provide useful information for diagnosing the problem.

Logs are often the first place to check when troubleshooting daemon issues. Daemons typically log important events, errors, and warnings to system logs. In Linux-based systems, these logs can be accessed through journalctl, which displays logs stored in the systemd journal.

By running journalctl -u <daemon_name>, administrators can view logs specific to a particular daemon, helping to identify error messages, warnings, or unusual behavior. For example, if a web server daemon like Apache or Nginx is not responding as expected, checking the error logs might reveal issues with file permissions, missing dependencies, or incorrect configurations. Similarly, daemon logs may indicate problems with network connectivity or resource exhaustion, such as insufficient memory or CPU overload, which can help guide the troubleshooting process.

Another important consideration when troubleshooting daemons is resource availability. Daemons often rely on system resources like memory, CPU, and disk space to perform their tasks. If a daemon is consuming too many resources, it may become unresponsive or fail to function properly. Using tools like top, htop, or ps, administrators can monitor the resource usage of running daemons and identify any that are using excessive memory or CPU. Resource limits can be adjusted using systemctl or configuration files to prevent daemons from overwhelming the system. For example, administrators can set memory and CPU limits in the unit files for systemd-managed daemons, ensuring that no single process can consume all available resources.

In some cases, issues arise when multiple daemons interact with each other. For example, a web server daemon might rely on a database daemon to handle client requests. If the database daemon is down or unresponsive, the web server might fail to serve requests, leading to service downtime. Similarly, if a network file system (NFS) share is mounted by a daemon, any issues with NFS, such as network connectivity problems or incorrect permissions, can prevent the daemon from accessing the necessary files. Troubleshooting these interactions involves understanding how the daemons communicate with each other and ensuring that the resources they depend on are available.

NFS is a common method for sharing files between systems in a network, and many daemons rely on NFS to access shared data. When troubleshooting NFS-related issues, it is important to check both the NFS server and the client configurations. On the server side, ensuring that the NFS export is correctly configured and accessible to the client is crucial. Administrators should verify that the /etc/exports file is correctly set up, specifying which directories are shared and which clients are allowed to access them. On the client side, checking that the NFS mount is correctly configured and that the client has the appropriate permissions is necessary. The command mount -t nfs <server>:<export> <mount_point> can be used to check the status of NFS mounts, while showmount -e <server> displays the available exports on the server.

One common issue with NFS is network connectivity. NFS relies on the network to mount and access shared directories, and any network-related issues can cause the NFS client to fail to connect to the server. Using tools like ping, traceroute, or netstat, administrators can diagnose network problems that may be affecting NFS performance. In addition, firewalls or network security settings may block the required ports for NFS, such as TCP/UDP ports 2049 and 111. Ensuring that the firewall allows traffic on these ports is crucial for NFS to function properly. When troubleshooting NFS, administrators should also ensure that the NFS server and client are running compatible versions of the protocol. NFSv3 and NFSv4, for example, have different features and configuration requirements, so mismatches between versions can cause issues.

Cron is another essential tool for automating system maintenance tasks, and it is frequently used in combination with daemons for tasks such as backups, log rotations, and system updates. When troubleshooting Cron, the first step is to verify that the Cron daemon is running properly. Using systemctl status cron or systemctl status crond, administrators can check the status of the Cron service. If the Cron daemon is not running, restarting it with systemctl restart cron can often resolve the issue.

If specific Cron jobs are not running as expected, administrators should check the Cron logs for error messages or missing output. Cron logs are typically stored in /var/log/cron, and reviewing these logs can reveal why a particular job failed. Common issues include incorrect paths to scripts or commands, permission issues, or environment variable mismatches. Since Cron jobs run in a minimal environment, ensuring that the job scripts reference full paths to commands and resources is crucial. Another potential issue is incorrect syntax in the crontab file. Cron uses a very specific syntax to define job schedules, and any errors in this syntax can prevent jobs from running. Using crontab -l to view the crontab file and ensuring that the scheduling syntax is correct can help resolve such issues.

One challenge when troubleshooting interactions between Cron, daemons, and NFS is dealing with timing-related problems. For instance, if a Cron job schedules a backup of an NFS-mounted directory, the job may fail if the NFS server is temporarily unavailable or if the network is slow. To mitigate this, administrators can add retry mechanisms to Cron job scripts, such as using a while loop to attempt the job multiple times before giving up. Another solution is to schedule backup jobs during off-peak hours when network load is lower, reducing the likelihood of NFS or network issues affecting the job.

Effective troubleshooting of daemons, NFS, and Cron requires a methodical approach and a solid understanding of how these components interact. By using diagnostic tools like systemctl, journalctl, and netstat, administrators can identify and resolve common issues related to daemon failures, NFS connectivity, and Cron job execution. Ensuring that all components are configured correctly, have the appropriate permissions, and are running in a stable environment is key to maintaining a well-functioning system.

Automating Daemon Management with Cron Jobs

Daemon management is a crucial part of system administration, especially when handling background processes that provide vital services such as web hosting, database management, and network services. Daemons often need to be started, stopped, restarted, or monitored at regular intervals to ensure the system remains stable, secure, and efficient. While many daemons are configured to start automatically at system boot through service management systems like systemd, there are times when administrators may need to automate additional aspects of daemon management. One of the most effective ways to automate these tasks is by using Cron, the time-based job scheduler in UNIX-like systems. By combining Cron jobs with daemon management tasks, administrators can automate a variety of system functions, such as checking daemon health, restarting failed services, and performing regular maintenance.

Cron jobs provide a simple but powerful way to schedule and automate tasks on a system. Cron is designed to execute scripts or commands at specific times or intervals, allowing system administrators to set up recurring tasks without needing to manually trigger them. When integrated with daemon management, Cron can be used to schedule a variety of tasks, including checking the status of daemons, restarting them if necessary, and even running custom scripts that address specific issues related to a daemon's operation. This automation reduces the administrative burden on system administrators, ensuring that critical tasks are consistently performed and that the system operates without interruption.

One of the most common use cases for Cron in daemon management is ensuring that daemons are running properly and restarting them if they fail. For example, a web server daemon such as Apache or Nginx may need to be restarted periodically to apply configuration changes, optimize performance, or address potential memory leaks. Instead of manually restarting the daemon, administrators can use Cron to automate this process. A Cron job can be scheduled to run a script every hour or every day to check whether the daemon is active. If the script detects that the daemon has stopped or is unresponsive, it can automatically restart the service to restore normal operation. This ensures that critical services are always available, reducing downtime and minimizing the need for manual intervention.

Cron can also be used to perform routine health checks on daemons. For instance, some daemons may log information about their status, performance, or errors to system logs or log files. Administrators can write a script that parses these logs for error messages or performance indicators that suggest the daemon is malfunctioning. By scheduling this script to run at regular intervals, administrators can receive notifications about any issues before they escalate. This proactive approach to monitoring can help detect problems early, ensuring that potential failures are addressed promptly. A script that checks log files for specific keywords or patterns can easily be scheduled using Cron to run every hour, ensuring that administrators are always informed about the health of their daemons.

Another important task that can be automated using Cron is the management of resources used by daemons. Daemons often consume system resources such as CPU, memory, and disk space. Over time, resource consumption may increase due to memory leaks, inefficient processes, or high demand on the system. Administrators can use Cron jobs to periodically monitor resource usage by daemons and take corrective action when necessary. For example, a Cron job can run a script that checks the memory usage of a specific daemon and alerts the administrator if it exceeds a predefined threshold. In some cases, it may even be possible to configure the script to automatically restart the daemon if resource usage becomes excessive, helping to prevent system slowdowns or crashes caused by resource exhaustion.

Cron can also help automate the cleanup of log files and temporary data generated by daemons. Daemons often produce log files that accumulate over time, taking up valuable disk space. This can lead to performance degradation or even cause the system to run out of disk space, potentially affecting the operation of other processes. By using Cron to schedule log rotation or cleanup tasks, administrators can ensure that log files do not grow uncontrollably. A Cron job can be configured to run a script that rotates logs, compresses old logs, or deletes outdated files at regular intervals, keeping disk usage under control and preventing logs from interfering with the operation of daemons or other system services.

Another useful way to combine Cron and daemon management is for backup automation. Many daemons, particularly database and web server daemons, handle critical data that must be backed up regularly. Rather than relying on manual backups, administrators can automate the process using Cron jobs. A Cron job can be scheduled to run backup scripts for important files, databases, or system configurations that daemons rely on. For example, administrators can use Cron to schedule daily backups of a database managed by a daemon, ensuring that data is regularly backed up without requiring constant oversight. This level of automation reduces the risk of data loss and ensures that critical backups are always up to date.

Cron can also be used to schedule the installation of updates or patches for daemons. Many daemons require periodic updates to fix bugs, improve performance, or address security vulnerabilities. Instead of manually checking for and installing updates, administrators can automate the process with Cron. A Cron job can be scheduled to run a script that checks for available updates, downloads them, and installs them during off-peak hours, ensuring that the system remains secure and up to date without disrupting normal operations. This is particularly useful in large environments where multiple daemons must be managed across many machines.

In more complex environments, administrators may use Cron to orchestrate the coordination of multiple daemons. For example, a daemon that handles user authentication may need to be restarted after a configuration change, while other services depend on this daemon to function properly. By using Cron to automate the restart of interdependent services, administrators can ensure that all relevant daemons are restarted in the correct order, minimizing the risk of service disruption. Cron jobs can also be used to trigger specific actions based on the status of one or more daemons. For example, if a database daemon fails, Cron could be used to restart the service and perform a database consistency check, ensuring that the service is fully operational before it accepts new requests.

Cron jobs are highly flexible and can be customized to fit the needs of any system, providing a powerful tool for automating daemon management. Whether checking the status of daemons, monitoring resource usage, or performing routine maintenance tasks, Cron helps to reduce the amount of manual intervention required, allowing system administrators to focus on higher-priority tasks. The ability to schedule and automate tasks at regular intervals not only improves the efficiency and reliability of system management but also ensures that critical services are continuously available and optimized. By combining Cron with daemon management, administrators can create a robust system that is both self-sustaining and capable of responding to issues quickly and automatically.

System Health Monitoring: Combining NFS, Sysctl, and Daemons

Maintaining the health and stability of a system is a crucial aspect of system administration. Ensuring that critical services remain operational, resources are efficiently managed, and performance is consistently optimized requires continuous monitoring and proactive intervention. A well-maintained system is one that can adapt to growing demands, troubleshoot issues before they become critical, and provide the necessary resources for both users and applications. A combination of tools such as NFS (Network File System), Sysctl, and daemons can play an integral role in system health monitoring, each contributing uniquely to the overall management of system resources, performance, and security.

NFS plays a fundamental role in modern system environments by enabling file sharing across different systems. In enterprise-level infrastructure, multiple machines often need to access shared directories, whether for collaborative purposes, data storage, or application support. NFS allows these machines to access files as if they were part of the local file system, making it essential for distributed systems. However, NFS introduces certain challenges when it comes to maintaining system health. If an NFS mount becomes unavailable or experiences issues, it can lead to downtime for applications or services that depend on the shared data.

When managing system health, administrators need to monitor NFS performance regularly to ensure that network file sharing remains reliable. One of the critical metrics for monitoring NFS health is the status of NFS mounts. Mounting issues can arise due to network problems, incorrect configurations, or permissions issues, all of which can disrupt the system's ability to access shared data. System administrators can set up daemons to periodically check the status of NFS mounts and verify connectivity between client machines and the NFS server. If a mount becomes stale or unresponsive, these daemons can trigger alerts or attempt to remount the NFS share automatically. By incorporating these checks into system health monitoring, administrators can minimize downtime and address potential issues before they impact users.

Another significant consideration when monitoring system health is resource utilization, which can affect performance and stability. Sysctl is an essential tool for managing kernel parameters that control various system behaviors, including memory management, process handling, and networking. By adjusting specific Sysctl parameters, administrators can optimize the system's resource management to prevent bottlenecks, improve efficiency, and enhance overall system stability. For example, adjusting the vm.swappiness parameter helps control how aggressively the kernel swaps memory pages to disk, which can prevent excessive swapping and improve system responsiveness.

Sysctl parameters also help administrators fine-tune network performance, an essential factor when NFS and other network-dependent services are involved. For instance, the net.ipv4.tcp_rmem and net.ipv4.tcp_wmem parameters define the minimum, default, and maximum sizes for TCP receive and send buffers. Tuning these parameters based on system and network load can optimize data transfer between the NFS server and clients, ensuring that file access over the network is smooth and efficient. Similarly, adjusting network congestion control algorithms and setting appropriate buffer sizes can reduce latency and prevent packet loss, which is critical when using NFS to share large files or handle heavy network traffic.

Sysctl can also be used to manage kernel security parameters that are crucial for maintaining system health. By adjusting settings related to network security, such as net.ipv4.conf.all.accept_source_route, administrators can prevent certain types of network attacks that might affect system stability or data integrity. Additionally, Sysctl settings related to process management, such as limiting the maximum number of file descriptors or controlling process limits, help maintain the system's health by preventing runaway processes or excessive resource consumption. These parameters ensure that daemons and other processes do not consume all available resources, which can degrade the performance of the entire system.

While Sysctl helps manage system resources and security, daemons provide ongoing monitoring and management of system services. Daemons are long-running processes that perform essential tasks, such as logging, monitoring system health, handling requests, and ensuring that critical services remain available. Many daemons are designed to run continuously, handling system maintenance and responding to events that require intervention. For example, a monitoring daemon could be configured to check the health of key services, such as the web server or database daemon, and automatically restart them if they fail. Similarly, a network monitoring daemon might be configured to track network traffic and resource usage, providing alerts when thresholds are exceeded or when connectivity issues arise.

By leveraging Sysctl and NFS alongside daemons, system administrators can create a robust monitoring framework that provides real-time insights into system performance, resource usage, and service availability. Daemons can be configured to monitor Sysctl parameters and system metrics, sending alerts when a parameter exceeds an acceptable range. For instance, a daemon could monitor memory usage and alert the administrator if swap usage exceeds a certain threshold, indicating potential memory pressure. Similarly, daemons can monitor the health of NFS mounts, ensuring that critical file systems are always available and performing optimally.

Daemons can also automate various system maintenance tasks, which is essential for maintaining a healthy system. For example, administrators can configure daemons to periodically clean up temporary files, rotate logs, or run backups at scheduled intervals. These tasks help keep the system running smoothly by preventing disk space exhaustion, ensuring that log files do not become too large, and protecting data from loss. When combined with Cron jobs, daemons can be scheduled to run maintenance tasks during off-peak hours, minimizing the impact on system performance and ensuring that essential services remain available to users.

The integration of Sysctl, NFS, and daemons in system health monitoring ensures that administrators have the tools they need to keep the system running efficiently and securely. Sysctl parameters provide fine-grained control over system resources, allowing administrators to tune network and memory settings to prevent bottlenecks and improve overall performance. NFS ensures that data is shared efficiently across systems, while daemons provide continuous monitoring and management of services, ensuring that the system remains responsive and reliable. By automating system maintenance tasks and integrating real-time monitoring, administrators can reduce the likelihood of system failures, improve resource allocation, and maintain optimal system health.

Effective system health monitoring requires not only proactive monitoring but also the ability to quickly identify and address issues. By combining Sysctl, NFS, and daemons, administrators can create a comprehensive and automated monitoring system that reduces the likelihood of downtime, prevents resource exhaustion, and ensures that system services are always available. These tools work together to maintain the health of the system, providing administrators with the insights and control they need to ensure the system performs at its best, even in demanding environments.

Best Practices for SysAdmin Tool Integration

System administration requires the seamless integration of various tools to maintain the efficiency, security, and stability of computer systems. From monitoring performance and managing resources to automating tasks and ensuring reliability, administrators need to leverage a diverse set of utilities. Among these, tools such as Sysctl, Cron, and various monitoring daemons are indispensable in achieving streamlined operations and efficient system management. When used together, these tools can automate routine tasks, optimize resource usage, and improve overall system health. To ensure the tools work together harmoniously, system administrators must follow best practices for integration. This chapter explores the key practices for integrating sysadmin tools effectively to build a robust, efficient, and reliable system.

The first key practice in integrating sysadmin tools is to understand the functionality of each tool and how they interact with each other. Sysctl, for example, allows administrators to configure kernel parameters that affect the performance and security of the system, such as memory management, networking, and process limits. Cron, on the other hand, is used to schedule tasks and automate system management processes at specific times or intervals, including running backups, rotating logs, or applying updates. Monitoring daemons, such as those used to check the status of system services or track system performance, are crucial for real-time system health checks. Understanding how each of these tools works individually and how they can complement each other is essential for effective integration.

One best practice for tool integration is to automate routine tasks using Cron jobs to trigger Sysctl configurations or monitoring daemons. Automating these processes reduces the need for constant manual intervention, ensuring that tasks are consistently performed at the right intervals. For example, Cron can be used to schedule the periodic execution of Sysctl commands that fine-tune kernel parameters. This ensures that any changes to system performance or security configurations are applied regularly, without requiring administrators to remember to manually adjust them. Similarly, Cron can schedule the execution of monitoring scripts or daemons that check the status of critical services, such as database servers or web servers, ensuring that these services remain functional and performing well.

Monitoring daemons themselves must be properly integrated with both Cron and Sysctl to be effective. These daemons often collect system metrics, such as CPU usage, memory consumption, disk space, and network performance. By integrating Sysctl, administrators can ensure that the kernel is configured optimally for the workload that the monitoring daemons are tracking. For example, if a daemon is monitoring system memory, it can be integrated with Sysctl to adjust the system's vm.swappiness or vm.dirty_ratio parameters for optimal memory management. This kind of integration ensures that the system is responsive under load and can handle heavy tasks without unnecessary swapping or resource exhaustion.

Another important best practice is to ensure proper configuration of logging and alerts for automated tasks. While Cron jobs, Sysctl commands, and daemons can automate numerous tasks, administrators must be able to track the success or failure of these tasks. Logs are crucial for troubleshooting and performance tuning. When a Cron job runs a Sysctl command or triggers a monitoring daemon, the results of these tasks should be logged to a file that can be reviewed periodically. Additionally, alerts should be configured so that administrators are notified when something goes wrong, such as when a daemon fails to start or a system parameter is set incorrectly. For example, if a Cron job is used to restart a service, the administrator should receive an alert if the service fails to restart after multiple attempts. By integrating logging and alerting mechanisms, administrators can proactively respond to potential issues before they disrupt system performance.

Incorporating Sysctl adjustments into system startup procedures is another best practice for integration. Sysctl parameters often need to be set early in the boot process, especially in systems that require specific memory, network, or process management settings to optimize performance. By integrating Sysctl adjustments into system startup scripts, administrators can ensure that the correct parameters are applied as soon as the system begins operating. For instance, parameters related to network performance, such as net.ipv4.tcp_rmem and net.ipv4.tcp_wmem, should be configured during system boot so that network daemons benefit from optimized settings immediately upon startup. Similarly, for security-critical configurations, such as enabling randomization of address space or controlling access to file systems, setting these parameters at startup ensures that the system operates securely from the moment it boots up.

Additionally, it is important to properly configure resource limits when integrating Sysctl and Cron with daemons. Daemons that run in the background consume system resources like memory, CPU, and disk space. Sysctl provides a variety of kernel parameters that allow administrators to limit the resources available to these daemons. For example, parameters such as kernel.pid_max can be configured to prevent excessive processes from being spawned, while fs.file-max limits the number of file handles that can be allocated. Cron jobs can schedule regular checks on these limits and adjust them based on system usage patterns or workloads. This integration ensures that daemons do not consume excessive resources, which can degrade system performance or cause other services to fail.

Furthermore, administrators must focus on the security of sysadmin tools during integration. Both Sysctl and Cron can modify critical system settings, and monitoring daemons often run with elevated privileges. Therefore, it is essential to restrict access to these tools to authorized users only. Using proper file and directory permissions ensures that sensitive configuration files, like those for Sysctl and Cron, are not tampered with by unauthorized users. Additionally, any scripts executed through Cron or monitoring daemons should be written with security in mind, avoiding insecure commands and ensuring that they do not expose the system to security vulnerabilities. Monitoring for unauthorized access or changes to configuration files is essential for maintaining system integrity and preventing malicious activities.

Finally, regular audits of sysadmin tool configurations are vital to ensure that they remain optimized and secure. Over time, system requirements change, and the parameters set in Sysctl or Cron may need to be adjusted. By auditing the configurations periodically, administrators can ensure that the tools are still performing as expected and that no misconfigurations have occurred. These audits can be automated using Cron jobs that regularly check system health, configurations, and resource limits, reporting any discrepancies or inefficiencies that need to be addressed.

The integration of Sysctl, Cron, and monitoring daemons allows system administrators to automate system management tasks, optimize performance, and ensure the stability of services. Best practices for integrating these tools involve understanding how each one functions, automating key tasks with Cron jobs, ensuring proper logging and alerting, and securing access to critical system tools. By carefully configuring and regularly auditing these tools, administrators can maintain a well-functioning system that is both efficient and secure, with minimal manual intervention required. The ability to integrate these tools effectively leads to streamlined system administration, fewer outages, and better overall system health.

www.ingramcontent.com/pod-product-compliance
Lightning Source LLC
LaVergne TN
LVHW022317060326
832902LV00020B/3519

* 9 7 9 8 2 8 1 8 9 5 5 5 2 *